Life
Below Stairs

TRUE LIVES OF
EDWARDIAN SERVANTS

ALISON MALONEY

Michael O'Mara Books Limited

This paperback edition first published in 2015

First published in Great Britain in 2011 by
Michael O'Mara Books Limited
9 Lion Yard
Tremadoc Road
London SW4 7NQ

A CIP catalogue record for this book is available from the British Library.

Papers used by Michael O'Mara Books Limited are natural, recyclable
products made from wood grown in sustainable forests. The
manufacturing processes conform to the environmental regulations of
the country of origin.

ISBN: 978-1-78243-435-1 in paperback print format
ISBN: 978-1-84317-781-4 in EPub format
ISBN: 978-1-84317-782-1 in Mobipocket format

1 2 3 4 5 6 7 8 9 10

Cover design by James Empringham
Designed and typeset by K.DESIGN, Winscombe, Somerset

Printed and bound by CPI Group (UK) Ltd, Croydon, CR0 4YY

www.mombooks.com

Life
Below Stairs

In loving memory of my grandparents,
Jean and Sandy Cook and Jim and Dorothy Tripp.
With love and thanks to Sally and Gill.

Afternoon

Contents

Introduction

IN THE TWENTY-FIRST century, domestic service is the domain of the few butlers, housekeepers and nannies who keep the richest homes in the country ticking over and usually command a high wage. But just one hundred years ago, service was the largest form of employment in the UK. The 1911 census showed that 1.3 million people in England and Wales worked 'below stairs' and many of those would have been in average middle-class homes, employed by doctors, lawyers and office clerks, rather than dukes and princes.

With millions of families living in stifling poverty in the Edwardian era, going into service was a sought-after alternative to near starvation but it was no easy option. From scullery maid to housekeeper and butler, the domestic servant was at the beck and call of their master and mistress every hour of the day. Up with the lark and toiling well into the night, they were rewarded with meagre wages and sparse, comfort-free accommodation in the attic or basement. While their employers dined on nine-course meals, costing up to six times a maid's annual wage, employees were treated to the leftover cold cuts in the basement kitchen. As the Edwardian upper classes organized their busy social calendars around the London season, the shooting season and weekend parties, the staff was lucky to get one day off a month.

But even as the more fortunate Edwardians basked in the lap of luxury, the winds of change were beginning to blow. Opportunities in shops, manufacturing and offices were offering young girls higher wages and more free time, the suffragette movement was filling the newspapers and the lower classes, who once 'knew their place', were beginning to demand more from their middle- and upper-class employers. 'The servant problem' was a frequent topic of conversation in society drawing rooms and politicians anxiously discussed what could be done to encourage more workers to choose domestic service. In 1914, the First World War saw the end of the golden age of domestic service. Life Below Stairs was soon to become a thing of the past.

TYPIST (LADY) WANTED. Must be a competent operator, with good knowledge of shorthand. Apply by letter only, stating age, experience, and salary required, to Millington and Sons, Limited, 32, Budge-row, E.C.

Domestic service was not the only option for young women

CHAPTER ONE

Social Background

URING THE CLASS-RIDDEN Victorian era, the social divide between rich and poor had become a chasm. By the turn of the century, poverty had reached shocking levels, especially in cities, and in his 1901 report on the slums of York the Quaker philanthropist Seebohm Rowntree concluded that 28 per cent of the population of the city was living in intolerable hardship. At the same time he concluded that 'the keeping of or not keeping of servants' was the defining line between the working classes and those of a superior social standing.

Domestic service, while arduous and all-consuming, provided a reasonable alternative to the slums and a certain amount of social status, and was taken up by a significant number of both sexes in Britain. A large percentage of women who worked were in service. The 1901 census showed that they numbered 1,690,686 women, or 40.5 per cent of the adult female working population.

Children, particularly girls, also made up a significant proportion of the lower posts in a large household and the higher up the social scale the employer, the more cachet was awarded to the positions in the house. Young girls would be looking for a post in a good home from the age of twelve or thirteen, and in some cases they started as young as ten. And while many of these came from the city slums, employers often preferred to take the children of rural families, who were considered to be more conscientious and hard-working than those from the cities.

Work was hard but maids were an essential addition to all homes from the lower middle classes upwards. In an age of few labour-saving appliances, the mistress of the house would struggle to run even an average-sized household on her own. An aristocratic seat or country house would require a large staff in order to run from day to day, while even a modest middle-class home would employ one or two servants.

At the turn of the century, however, things were beginning to change, at least for the professional classes. In his 1904 publication *The English House*, German architect Hermann Muthesius said that many middle-class families complained that, with new opportunities for working women in shops and offices, '£20 maids', those who earned around £20 annually, were hard to come by. That, along with the introduction of household appliances over the coming years, led to a decline in domestic staff and a rethink of the architecture of middle-income homes. Houses became smaller, cosier and more manageable for a housewife and, after the First World War, staff were to be found in the wealthier households alone.

In the years leading up to the war, a family's social standing was heavily dependent on the number of staff it could afford to employ, as this was an obvious indication of wealth. Many of the richer families would employ up to twenty staff and, in the larger aristocratic homes, it often increased to thirty or forty. At the Duke of Westminster's country seat, Eaton Hall in Cheshire, there were over three hundred servants, although this was an exceptionally large number, even amongst the aristocracy.

Eaton Hall in Cheshire

The 6th Marquess of Bath was born in 1905 at Longleat, a vast rolling estate in Wiltshire, and died in 1992. As a child he had his own valet and his parents employed a total of forty-three indoor staff. In 1973, when he and his wife were making do with two servants, a resident married couple who performed the duties of butler, cook, housekeeper and maid, he looked back on the servant age with some nostalgia.

'I think the more servants one had the better,' he recalled in *Not in Front of the Servants: A True Portrait of Upstairs, Downstairs Life*. 'We had two lampboys, two steward boys and about five footmen. You were looked after in the lap of luxury. If you ask me whether I'd like to go back to those days, of course I would. Obviously one would, because it was all so much more for us, but I'm not complaining, because times have changed. It's so different from the old days when people were brought up to be in domestic service.'

Lady Lindsay of Dowhill, otherwise known as Loelia, Duchess of Westminster, was born in 1902 and recalled in her 1961 memoirs, *Grace and Favour*, how they were considered 'dreadfully badly off', despite her father being a respected courtier to Edward VII. The main reason for this 'shame' was that the Palace pay only stretched to five maids, a manservant, a boy and two gardeners. This led to embarrassment in their social circle who were 'mostly people who had too many servants to count and who owned stately homes'.

So intense was the pressure to keep up with the Joneses in late Victorian and early Edwardian households that many middle-class mistresses deprived themselves of expensive food and basic needs in order to maintain the illusion of wealth through the number of servants employed. The Victorian author

William Makepeace Thackeray described this phenomenon in his satirical novel *The Book of Snobs*. The character Lady Susan Scraper feeds herself and her two daughters such meagre rations that they fill up on buns.

> *For the fact is, that when the footmen, and the ladies' maids, and the fat coach-horses, which are jobbed [rented], and the six dinner-parties in the season, and the two great solemn evening-parties, and the rent of the big house, and the journey to an English or foreign watering-place for the autumn, are paid, my lady's income has dwindled away to a very small sum, and she is as poor as you or I.*

Of course, very few mistresses would go as far as starving themselves for the privilege of keeping more servants but Thackeray's thrifty character illustrates the importance of staff when it came to keeping up appearances and boosting status.

Equally, in the early 1900s, the more staff you had, the easier it was to employ more as the dwindling number of young men and women willing to go into domestic work preferred the more well-to-do households. An elevated social position for an employer meant their servants automatically gained respect from the local population, including the tradesmen and shop workers. More staff also meant companionship below stairs, whereas a lone housemaid, moving away from her family for the first time, would feel isolated and lonely in her new home.

Mrs G. Edwards recalled in *Lost Voices of the Edwardians* leaving her Brixton home at fifteen to become an under-nurse at a house in Wetherby Gardens in London's Kensington. 'I only went back to my home in Brixton about once a fortnight, for an afternoon off. I used to get very homesick. I missed my home but my mother said I must stay for a year so I could get a character reference.'

In *Life Below Stairs in the Twentieth Century* by Pamela Horn another teenager, who travelled from Norwich to Beckenham to become a maid, recalled writing to her mother to say, 'I wouldn't mind what I done at home, if only she'd let me come. She wrote back and said be thankful you've got a bed to lie on and a good meal.'

Even the more aristocratic homes were beginning to cut back by the turn of the century. Wages were getting higher and taxation on the wealthy, especially the death duties introduced in 1894, were diminishing the upper-class pot. Education had become free to all from 1890 and the 1902 Balfour Act extended the school leaving age from ten to twelve, leading to a sharp decline in young children going into service. The suffragette movement was turning the heads of young women, who were choosing secretarial courses or shop positions over a lifetime of servitude, and the First World War, followed by the Depression, was to change the social order for ever. The Edwardian era was about to see the sun set on the last golden age of the upstairs-downstairs household.

CHAPTER TWO

Household Structure

UPSTAIRS, DOWNSTAIRS

THE UPPER-CLASS and upper-middle-class Edwardian household had a very strict hierarchy and each servant was expected to know their place. The staff, particularly the longest-serving members, may well have formed a bond with the family but the line between 'upstairs' and 'downstairs' was never blurred. Domestic staff could not aspire to live the lives of their employers and even the most senior would be aware that over-familiarity or a word out of turn would never do.

Diarist and author Lady Cynthia Asquith wrote that 'no one from Upstairs was required to lend a hand at the sink – not even once a week. Indeed, no such invasion of the Staff's territory would have been tolerated.'

The staff quarters and the family quarters were separated by a large door that was often covered in green baize. Each servant was aware of exactly which rooms past that door they were allowed to enter and when, and few would have dared to stray outside their given parameters.

DOWNSTAIRS, DOWNSTAIRS

In large houses, the household staff, responsible for the cleaning and laundry, was presided over by the housekeeper. The serving staff would be under the butler and the kitchen staff would answer to the cook. However, there was some crossover between the housekeeper and the cook, as the former was generally in charge of jams, pickles and confectionery while the latter presided over the meals.

Although the Edwardian era saw the rise of the suffragettes, and women servants outnumbered men by three to one, life below stairs was still a male-dominated hierarchy with a butler or manservant given greater authority, and therefore higher pay, than a housekeeper. This also meant that the ability to maintain a manservant or butler was looked upon as an enviable badge of wealth.

In *What the Butler Saw* E.S. Turner writes, 'As often as not, he was kept for ostentation and sometimes for intimidation. He was expected to be deferential to his superiors and haughty towards his inferiors, which included his master's inferiors.'

In smaller households, where no butler was employed, the housekeeper was the undisputed ruler of the 'downstairs' staff. She was the link between the mistress of the house and the lowliest of maids. In her *Book of Household Management* Mrs Beeton explains:

> *AS SECOND IN COMMAND IN THE HOUSE, except in large establishments, where there is a house steward, the housekeeper must consider herself as the immediate representative of her mistress, and bring, to the management of the household, all those qualities of honesty, industry, and vigilance, in the same degree as if she were at the head of her own family.*
>
> *Constantly on the watch to detect any wrong-doing on the part of any of the domestics, she will overlook all that goes on in the house, and will see that every department is thoroughly attended to, and that the servants are comfortable, at the same time that their various duties are properly performed.*

As well as the indoor staff, there would be a head gardener with, in larger houses, four or five groundsmen under him, and possibly a coachman, who would take charge of the stables and supervise the grooms. However, as more households splashed out on newfangled motor cars throughout the first decade of the twentieth century, many coachmen were replaced with chauffeurs who also acted as car mechanics.

For wealthier families, this pattern would be repeated in more than one house, with many boasting a London home, a country seat and often a sporting estate, used for the shooting season and weekend parties, in Scotland or Ireland.

THE HIERARCHY OF A HOUSE

Bottom of the ladder

The maid-of-all-work was the lowliest of all the servants and was often a child of twelve or thirteen. She could be the sole servant of a middle-class family or at the bottom rung of a larger ladder in a big household. Up with the lark, she would be rushed off her feet until bedtime and her endless lists of tasks would be menial and fairly degrading. The children, who came from very poor families or straight from the workhouse, were often mistreated by mistresses or superior staff and, more often than not, would have nowhere to turn to seek solace.

Even Mrs Beeton had a pang of sympathy for the downtrodden 'general maid'.

> *The general servant, or maid-of-all-work, is perhaps the only one of her class deserving of commiseration: her life is a solitary one, and, in some places, her work is never done. She is also subject to rougher treatment than either the house or kitchen maid, especially in her earlier career.*

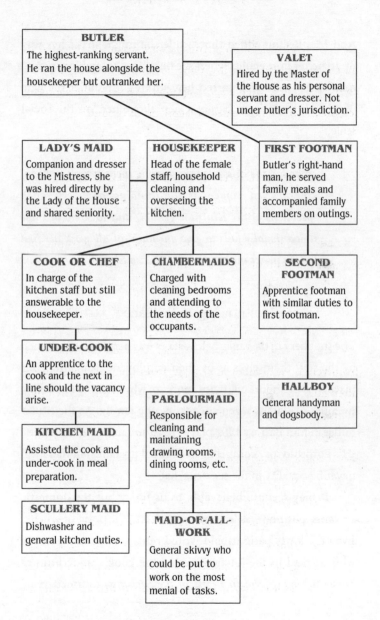

BUTLER
The highest-ranking servant. He ran the house alongside the housekeeper but outranked her.

VALET
Hired by the Master of the House as his personal servant and dresser. Not under butler's jurisdiction.

LADY'S MAID
Companion and dresser to the Mistress, she was hired directly by the Lady of the House and shared seniority.

HOUSEKEEPER
Head of the female staff, household cleaning and overseeing the kitchen.

FIRST FOOTMAN
Butler's right-hand man, he served family meals and accompanied family members on outings.

COOK OR CHEF
In charge of the kitchen staff but still answerable to the housekeeper.

CHAMBERMAIDS
Charged with cleaning bedrooms and attending to the needs of the occupants.

SECOND FOOTMAN
Apprentice footman with similar duties to first footman.

UNDER-COOK
An apprentice to the cook and the next in line should the vacancy arise.

PARLOURMAID
Responsible for cleaning and maintaining drawing rooms, dining rooms, etc.

HALLBOY
General handyman and dogsbody.

KITCHEN MAID
Assisted the cook and under-cook in meal preparation.

SCULLERY MAID
Dishwasher and general kitchen duties.

MAID-OF-ALL-WORK
General skivvy who could be put to work on the most menial of tasks.

And Mrs Beeton added that, while she might make her way up to better households when she became a 'tolerable servant', many a general maid started her working life under the wife of a small tradesman, barely a step above her 'on the social scale':

> *Although the class contains among them many excellent, kind-hearted women, it also contains some very rough specimens of the feminine gender, and to some of these it occasionally falls to give our maid-of-all-work her first lessons in her multifarious occupations.*

Knowing Your Place

The snobbery in the ranks below stairs was perpetuated as much by the staff themselves as by their employers. 'Knowing your place' was as important, if not more so, when talking to a fellow member of staff as when addressing the family. As the titular butler in J.M. Barrie's 1902 play, *The Admirable Crichton*, states, 'His Lordship may compel us to be equal upstairs, but there will never be equality in the servants' hall.'

It may seem unbelievable to us today but the domestic servants' position was jealously guarded to the point of cruelty. Even the lowly parlourmaid would refuse to speak to anyone who worked in the kitchen, seeing the cook's underlings as beneath her. In *Not in Front of the Servants*, fourteen-year-old scullery maid Beatrice Gardner remembered a particularly nasty trick played on her by one such 'superior'.

> *I well remember having to carry cans of hot water up many flights of stairs when her ladyship was changing for dinner, and being met en route by one of the housemaids who with a straight face said that I must also take a certain china article (used in the days of no bathrooms) and hand this to her lady in her room, together with a can of hot water. This I duly did and to my utter dismay, received a month's notice for being 'rude and insolent', which was really funny when I think how terrified I was to even speak to anyone. But of course no one knew it was the fault of this wretched housemaid, playing a trick on a child who had just left home.*

The Nursery

As well as these basic staff, the presence of children in the household would require still further staffing. A nanny would preside over the care of youngsters and under her were a few junior nurses or nursemaids, often children themselves, to take on the everyday care of babies and infants.

In the 1871 census, almost 20 per cent of nurses in full-time domestic service were under the age of fifteen. In fact, 710 girls in the job were under the age of ten.

A fully fledged nanny, who ran the nursery, was ranked high enough on the social scale to have another member of staff waiting on her, usually called a nursery maid. Nanny was not expected to wash up a plate or cup or tidy the nursery, and the menial tasks, such as warming milk, were left to the nurse. Even though the youngsters saw no one but the nanny and the children all day, they were not permitted to mix with the ordinary domestic staff.

Serving the Children

Mrs G. Edwards became an under-nurse in Kensington at 15.

The head nurse was above me. I called her 'Nurse' and she called me by my Christian name. The house had a cook, a kitchen maid, a housemaid, a parlourmaid, a coachman and a groom. My job involved attending to the children. I got up at six o'clock to walk the children's dog round the square. Then I went downstairs to fetch anything for the children. I used to take their shoes and boots to be cleaned in the kitchen. The children lived in the nursery and we had our food sent up to us, but sometimes the two eldest children went down to dine with the family and I would go down with them to serve them. I stood in the dining room with them.

Max Arthur, *Lost Voices of the Edwardians*

Playtime in the nursery

The Governess

In the Victorian era, older children, especially girls who would not be sent away to boarding school, required a governess. By the turn of the century, with many girls now getting a formal education, fewer and fewer families were employing governesses.

Although a paid member of staff, the governess would have come from a similar social class as her employers and she was not considered a servant as such. As she would need to be educated, the majority were unmarried daughters of middle-class or well-to-do families who, for one reason or another, needed to support themselves or simply wanted to work. Being too genteel to consider work as a servant, they entered the house in a social limbo. They were often scorned by the servants who saw their elevated status as unfair and may well have been looked down on by the family, who would see a woman's need to work as an indication of her family's failure.

OUTDOORS STAFF

Land Steward

Only to be found on the larger estates, which included farmland or tithe cottages, the land steward was more employee than servant and was responsible for managing the rents and keeping the business profitable. He was well educated, highly paid and lived in a house on the estate, so his social status was closer to that of the family itself and he would be in charge of hiring and firing outdoor staff.

The Gardener

The head gardener was considered 'upper staff' and on a par with the housekeeper in the hierarchy. Although this meant higher wages and good living conditions, his position as outdoor help meant he was separate from the upper servants of the house.

SITUATIONS WANTED.

A LADY wishes to recommend a boy, aged 15, to be under a gardener in a gentleman's family; willing to be useful; three years' excellent character.—B. Etterick, Putney Common.

The job of under-gardener was seen as a valuable position for a young boy

In smaller houses the gardener might have worked alone or with one under-gardener but in the larger country houses and stately homes he would have had a formidable workforce. For example, at the Buckinghamshire mansion of Waddesdon Hall, owned by the hugely wealthy Rothschild family at the turn of the century, the head gardener tended the vast gardens with a staff of six under-gardeners.

The Stable Master

Like the head gardener, the head groom or stable master was ranked with the 'upper staff', although he would not have been afforded all their privileges. Depending on the size of the house, he would have presided over several grooms and stable boys, some of whom started as young as ten.

Coachmen

Although cars were becoming fashionable in the Edwardian era, most families still relied on horse-drawn carriages and it was the coachmen's task to keep them in good working order and pristine at all times. They were also responsible for cleaning the tack, although this job might have been delegated depending on how many stable hands were employed. The coachmen ranked above the grooms.

DAILY DUTIES

The Valet

Although he commanded as much respect as the butler, the master's personal valet had no staff directly under him. His sole responsibility was to tend to the master's needs, such as his wardrobe and toilette. He would rise before his employer and go to bed after him, so he needed to be able to survive on little sleep.

Every day he would ensure that the correct outfit for each occasion was pressed and ready to be worn and that his master's shoes and boots were clean and polished, often with newly ironed shoelaces. In the morning he would shave his employer, sometimes using a shaving soap or balm of his own recipe, and he would make sure a bath was drawn when his master demanded it.

Manny Lane

Minnie Lane's brother Manny had always wanted to be a gentleman's valet and found a position at a house in Manchester. After a three-month absence the family heard a knock at the window at four o'clock one Sunday morning as the prodigal son returned, complete with a northern accent. 'We asked him why he'd come home and he said the gentleman he worked for wanted him to cut his toenails, and he wouldn't do it. He'd do a lot of things but he wouldn't do that.'

Max Arthur, *Lost Voices of the Edwardians*

A valet had special standing in the household, treated as a close friend and confidant of the head of the household. On shooting days on larger estates he might be responsible for looking after the guns and loading his master's weapon, unless there was a 'loader' or under-keeper to take that role, and on outings he would take charge of train timetables and travel arrangements, as well as supervise the packing of suitcases. He would travel with his master, often abroad, and would even act as a translator and tour guide on the trips, sorting out any problems that arose through ignorance of local customs.

In order to procure all the goods and services required, a top valet would be phenomenally well connected and discreet, rather like the best hotel porters of today. The famous fictional valet Jeeves, created by P.G. Wodehouse in 1915, is the perfect example of the invaluable 'fixer', able to lay his hands on whatever his master, Bertie Wooster, requires at short notice and capable of helping him out of any tight spot.

As well as a top-end salary, the valet received many tips and gifts, and would often be given unwanted clothes to sell or wear himself. In fact, many made enough money to go into the hotel business, or open high-end stores. Lord Byron's valet James Brown and his wife Sarah became the founders of the famous Brown's Hotel, in Mayfair.

By the Edwardian era, as servant numbers reduced in all but the biggest households, dedicated valets were becoming rare, with many of their duties being taken on by the butler.

The Lady's Maid

Like the valet, the lady's maid was a luxury few could afford but, for those with the means, she became a trusted and valued companion. Her duties were somewhere between dresser and secretary and she needed to be well versed in the latest fashions, charged as she was with keeping her mistress up to date with elegant trends. In fact, in the Victorian era, when they had been more numerous, French ladies' maids became something of a status symbol because they were thought to know more about the Parisian designs.

The lady's maid would look after the wardrobe, help her mistress choose dresses for each occasion, and help her with her hair and make-up. With some society ladies changing up to five times a day for various engagements, this was a full-time job in itself. She would also be on hand to suggest lotions and beauty enhancements to stem the march of time, and help with the brimming social calendar. In large houses, she would be the only person permitted to enter the lady's boudoir, forbidden ground even for the master of the house.

Although they were invariably young, with the majority leaving to marry by the time they were in their mid-twenties, ladies maids enjoyed a senior position similar to that of the valet. This meant they were regarded with some suspicion and even hatred by the lower staff, because they had the ear and the trust of the mistress.

They too would receive perks in the shape of cast-off dresses and beauty products, and many developed airs and graces above their station, objecting strongly if asked to attend to any other female. A Victorian guide entitled *The Lady's Maid* warned them against such pretensions and urged them to bear in mind that their elevated position, better clothes and 'seat in the dressing room and on your master's carriage' were merely temporary perks of the job. 'Your heart should still be where your station is – among the poor; so that if you have to return to your old ways of living when your years of service are over, you may not feel hurt or degraded but as if you were returning home.'

The Butler

During the Victorian era the butler had seen his position elevated by the paring down of household staff. The house steward, once his superior, had almost disappeared and valets were retained only by the wealthiest of families, leaving the butler to tend to the master of the house and to run the domestic staff.

The butler oversaw the running of the household and was directly in charge of the serving staff, footmen and hall staff and, therefore, held responsible for their conduct. In addition, he would liaise with the housekeeper on the duties and conduct of the kitchen and household staff. He ran the extensively stocked wine cellar, polished the family silver and oversaw the smooth running of all meals, keeping a watchful eye on the footmen waiting at table to make sure they observed the correct etiquette. When guests were being entertained, he would oversee the menu and choose the wine, filling the glasses himself.

At lunch he might serve the meal alone, as the footmen were often otherwise engaged, and at dinner he was required .

Keeping a watchful eye

to set the starter on the table before calling in the family. Mrs Beeton observed that:

> *He carries in the first dish, and announces in the drawing room that dinner is on the table, and respectfully stands by the door until the company are seated, when he takes his place behind his master's chair on the left, to remove the covers, handing them to the other attendants to carry out. After the first course of plates is supplied, his place is at the sideboard to serve the wines, but only when called on.*

As a mark of respect the other members of staff always addressed the butler as 'sir'.

The Housekeeper

The duties of a housekeeper, and the meaning of the term, varied widely depending on whether she was employed in a middle-class home or a 'big house'. Widowed or single men of means often had a housekeeper who would provide the most basic functions of a housewife, keeping the home clean, cooking meals, looking after children and, in some cases, even sharing the bed.

In wealthy households, however, the housekeeper was the head of the domestic staff, and would run the establishment with military precision. She was in charge of the kitchen staff and the maids and was assisted in her domination by the cook and, in some instances, by the head housemaid. According to the 1825 householders' bible, *The Complete Servant*, she should be 'a steady middle-aged woman, of great experience in her profession and a tolerable knowledge of the world'. The description was as relevant at the turn of the century as it was when it was written.

One of her most important duties was to greet the master and mistress when they returned home from a journey, or even a day out, by standing at the top of the main staircase or inside the front door. She would also greet weekend guests in order to show them to their rooms. She invariably jangled with the many keys attached to her waist, as she controlled the storerooms, china cupboards and linen cupboards and carried keys for all of the rooms in the building. She kept the household accounts and oversaw orders to tradesmen. She was also the sole keeper of the 'still-room' where the preserves, fruit wines and cordials were kept.

The housekeeper was addressed as 'Mrs' regardless of marital status and often inspired more fear from the 'unders' than the mistress or the butler. In his memoirs Albert Thomas, who went on to become a butler at Brasenose College, Oxford, recalled having to wash the butler's gout-stricken feet during his time as a footman to the Duke of Norfolk. Afterwards he joked to the other servants that he was pleased the old man wasn't a centipede, so unpleasant had been his task, but his jocular remark was overheard by the tyrannical housekeeper. He wrote, 'I would rather his grace had heard us, he was human, but her, Oh Lor' we did cop it.'

The 6th Marquess of Bath remembered being intimidated by one formidable lady in his father's employ at Longleat:

'Everyone, including us, was terrified of the housekeeper, Mrs Parker, dead a long time now, I'm afraid,' he revealed. 'She would go round the house running her fingers along the tops of the shelves to see that they were dusted. The housemaids used to tremble.'

Housemaids

In the best houses both chambermaids and parlourmaids would be employed, as well as 'between-stairs maids' or 'tweenies', who performed tasks in both the kitchen and the rest of the house, and the lowly maid-of-all-work. Parlourmaids were responsible for the reception rooms of the house, such as the drawing room, dining room, morning room and library, should there be one. She would dust and sweep each day, clear out the grates and light the fire in each room. She would also wash woodwork, clean lamps and polish tables in the rooms. The chambermaid had similar duties in the bedrooms, beginning each day by taking buckets of hot water and tea trays to the family and the guests, then lighting the fires, making the bed, cleaning the bedrooms and dusting under the bed.

As staffs shrunk in the early twentieth century, however, the two jobs were combined in the title 'housemaid', so that the duties overlapped. If the family could afford it, there may have been a first, second and third housemaid, with their ranks made clear in their titles. The lower housemaids would clean the rooms of those above them. Margaret Thomas was employed as a kitchen maid and, even though she was below the parlour-maids, she still outranked the lowest of the housemaids.

'I learned there was a footman as well as a butler [...] I had their bedroom to keep clean, which was in the basement,' she recounted in *The Day Before Yesterday* edited by Noel Streatfeild. 'My own bedroom was at the top of the house but the under housemaid cleaned it. I only had to make my bed.'

The Cook

There were two types of cook to be found in the kitchen of the grander homes – professed cooks and plain cooks. The professed cook was an expert at creating the fine dining experience the upper-class employers needed for entertaining but would not turn her hand to general kitchen work or even 'plain cooking', and had the ingredients prepared in advance by a kitchen maid or under-cook. The plain cook was often kept on for the day-to-day meals and for cooking for the servants. For families who could only afford one cook, an all-rounder was sought but not always found. Margaret Thomas remembered one household where she was employed as a kitchen maid but was surprised to find her duties included cooking for dinner parties. 'This I discovered was because she [the cook] could only do plain cooking and so had always employed a kitchen maid who could cook.'

The cook was absolute ruler in the territory of the kitchen and some were just as tyrannical as many housekeepers. At fourteen, Londoner Beatrice Gardner worked for a cook who made her polish the kitchen range with a piece of velvet to give it a perfect shine. 'I used to run and hide in the coalhouse if I upset any milk or gravy. Her rage had to be seen to be believed.'

As well as preparing the main meals, the cook would come up with a daily menu that was then presented to the mistress of the house for approval or alteration. Between mealtimes she would make jams and preserves, pastries and soups in advance.

Kitchen and Scullery Maids

The kitchen maid was a cook's closest assistant, and was employed to prepare all the ingredients before she started preparing the meal. She would chop vegetables, herbs and any meat that needed to be cut. She would also help with cooking, perhaps by boiling vegetables, preparing coffee and easier items such as toast, and she would often be expected to cater for the servants while the cook concentrated on the many courses to go upstairs.

She would cut sandwiches for tea and, if no scullery maid were employed, would also be responsible for the washing-up.

Even when the family were not entertaining, a large breakfast was followed by a hearty lunch and a dinner of many courses with tea in between. There may also have been soup or snacks at eleven in the morning and sandwiches in the late evening, so there was plenty of work to keep the cook and the kitchen maid busy all day.

While the kitchen maid contributed to the cooking, the scullery maid, where there was one, was charged with cleaning the kitchen and washing up. She would light the kitchen fires in the morning and sweep the floors, clean the range and the flues and heat the hot water for cooking.

Lily's Story

Lily Graham was put into an orphanage in 1900, at the age of seven, after the death of her father. At eleven, Lily was sent out to work in order to earn enough money to buy her maid's uniform and spent two years as a messenger and general helper at a dressmakers'. By 1908, she had saved enough money for her blue cotton dresses, white aprons and caps and she went into service as a scullery maid in Mayfair. She rose at 5.30 a.m. to scrub the floors, clean and light the kitchen range and she toiled until nine or ten in the evening. She was 13 and she was paid just £6 a year.

Frank Dawes, *Not in Front of the Servants*

Footmen

In the age of the carriage, footmen had been an essential part of every rich household and many houses employed three or four. Dressed in high livery, a footman would accompany the mistress on her afternoon outing, holding the carriage door for her, helping her avoid muddy puddles and carrying any parcels and purchases. He would also leave her in the carriage while he called to see if the lady she wished to visit was in, and if not would leave a calling card. A second would accompany the master as he went about his business and a third, if there was one, stayed at home to open the door to any callers, or to run errands for the family. A typical task would be to relay messages from one house to another, or to call on another household to ask after the family within and send his employer's regards. In the evening he would wait on the table at dinner, under the watchful eye of the butler. As liveried footmen were an indication of wealth, the grandest homes had many more than four. At Woburn Abbey, the family seat of the Duke of Bedford, a footman would stand behind each chair in the dining room, no matter how big the occasion. The biography of Mary Du Caurroy, who was Duchess of Bedford in the Edwardian period, observes:

> *Everything was done in splendid, if flamboyant, style. Liveried servants were evident in large numbers. Breakfast was served at ten each morning [...] Herbrand (the Duke) insisted on retaining all the ancient traditions of the house,*

he continued to ensure that every guest was provided with
his or her own gold teapot.

By the beginning of the twentieth century, however, many of the footman's functions had become obsolete because of two new inventions. The motor car, increasingly popular among the upper classes, meant the groom and footman were replaced with a single chauffeur on journeys, and the telephone made the carrying of messages about town unnecessary. Nonetheless some footmen were still kept on in a more ornamental role, more as an ostentatious show of wealth than a useful addition to the household. They were used to wait on tables as well as performing general tasks such as carrying coal, cleaning silver, announcing visitors and retrieving coats as dinner guests left. Some were given to the sons of the household to act as a personal assistant, like their fathers' valets, or performed the same duties for guests who arrived without their own valet.

Bizarrely, they were often given a generic name, such as William or James, which would be used for every footman employed by the household.

Hallboys

Like the maid-of-all-work, the hallboy came at the bottom of the pecking order and was the servant to the servants. He would not set foot in the main house during the course of his duties and would be at the beck and call of the butler and the footmen at all times. In his memoir, *Green Baize Door,* Ernest King said he went into domestic service at the very bottom, in a well-to-do north Devon house, and he spent all his time there waiting on the other staff. He had 'the table in the servants' hall to lay, the staff cutlery to clean and the staff meals to put on the table. In the butler's pantry I spent most of my time at the washing up tub.'

Other duties included cleaning the boots of the family's men as well as those of the butler and footmen and cleaning the kitchen knives.

The position of a hallboy, or houseboy, could be taken by a local lad who still lived with his parents, as Frank Honey recalled in *Lost Voices of the Edwardians.* Working at the house of an army captain in Canterbury, he was expected to turn up at six in the morning to start his chores. 'My first job was to groom two big black retrievers they had and then I had to let them out into the garden. Then I used to have to chop the wood and clean the shoes, the knives and the forks. There was no stainless steel cutlery in those days. We used to use brick dust.'

CHAPTER THREE

Pay and Conditions

PAY PACKETS AND PERKS

IN 1899, THE average yearly wage of a housemaid, aged between twenty-one and twenty-five, was found to be £16 5s., the equivalent of £927 today. A younger maid would earn considerably less, perhaps starting on £10 a year, £570 in current value. While this seems a remarkably small sum, it must be remembered that servants had little need, and even less time, to spend any money. Every position came with bed and board, so there were no bills to pay, and unless an employer was exceptionally mean, there was a plentiful supply of food and drink.

With a sixteen-hour day, and only one afternoon off a week, there was little time to spend their hard-earned cash and much of the money they received went back to their often poverty-stricken families. Many a young girl scrubbed her

fingers to the bone, year in year out, to put food on the table
for younger siblings or even just to keep dad in gin!

Servants were paid quarterly, sometimes annually, and
rarely was a penny paid in advance, so the youngsters in their
first job had a while to wait before they saw the spoils. Despite
the meagre amount, breakages and any items they needed to
buy throughout the year, such as stockings and shoes, were
deducted on payday.

Yearly Wages in 1901, with Today's Equivalent

	Wage 1901	Value 2011
Butler	£60	£3423
Housekeeper	£45	£2567
Cook	£40	£2282
Lady's maid	£32	£1826
Kitchen maid	£24	£1370
First footman	£26	£1484
Second footman	£24	£1370
First housemaid	£28	£1598
Second housemaid	£22	£1255
Scullery maid	£12	£685
Coachman	£18	£1027
Hallboy	£16	£913

Figures from *Report on Changes in Rates of Wages and Hours of Labour
in the U.K., with Comparative Statistics for 1900-1908* [1910 Cd.5324]

VITAL STATS

The pay structure wasn't always straightforward, however, and money was often decided on more than experience. The lady's maid, for example, was expected to be young so if she hit her mid-twenties and was still employed, her annual salary began to decrease.

Footmen, on the other hand, increased in value with every inch of height as the liveried uniform was considered to look smarter on the taller man. An extra premium was paid for two who were similar in stature and appearance. A matching pair of six-footers was considered quite a catch so was worth a few pounds more than the manservant of average proportion. They were often trained to act in unison, standing either side of a hallway or both accompanying a mistress on her visits.

In 1849 a letter to the magazine *Sidney's Emigrant Journal* asked for advice on this very issue. 'I am twenty-four years of age, a native of Scotland, and at present a gentleman's servant; but as I am not a six-foot man, nor particularly handsome, I have not the best chance of succeeding here.' He added that he had a reasonable education, great body strength and the capacity to withstand any climate, and asked whether he would do well in Australia or America. The magazine's adviser urged him to try Australia, where he could rise 'from man to master' and warned that 'service is considered rather degrading in America'.

In *The Life and Labour of the People of London*, published at the turn of the century, Charles Booth recorded the sliding scale of a footman's wages thus:

2nd footman, 5 ft 6 in.: £20–£22;   5 ft 10 in. to 6 ft: £28–£30
1st footman,   5 ft 6 in.: Up to £30; 5 ft 10 in. to 6 ft: £32–£40.

This height-conscious attitude was by no means confined to the footmen, although they bore the brunt of it.

Butler Eric Horne, author of *What the Butler Winked*, bemoaned the fact that he would never 'hope to attain the top of the tree' because he was only 5 ft 9 in., and in some houses even the maids were passed over for promotion to parlourmaid because they weren't tall enough.

FOOD AND BEER ALLOWANCE

As well as their wages, each employee was granted meat and sugar rations and a daily beer allowance according to their gender and rank in the household. In the majority of houses the food portions were generous with a typical allowance being 1½ lb of meat a day plus 1 lb of tea and 4 lb of sugar per month. Supper was usually comprised of the family's leftovers and dinner parties meant more delicacies to feast on 'below stairs'.

The etiquette manual *Cassell's Household Guide*, issued in 1880 and still used by the mistresses of the Edwardian era, advised employers that the provision of food and beer was more satisfactory than cash payments to cover food and drink:

> *For some reason or other, which it is difficult to account for, many housekeepers do not undertake to find grocery and beer, but allow money for those articles of consumption. Either such things are necessary to the diet of servants, or they are not. If they are necessary, it is better by far to provide tea, sugar, and beer, than to give money, which may not be applied to its proper use. In point of economy, the money payment is a losing one, because a housekeeper having to feed a certain number of persons daily, the better all the meals are supplied, the more regular is the consumption likely to be. A girl that goes without a good tea is more likely to prove an inordinate supper-eater than one who has previously enjoyed a good meal.*
>
> *With regard to beer money. If beer be a necessary, the money ought to be spent in buying the required nourishment; if not, there is no sense in giving wages in lieu of it.*

In a household where the family was away a lot, perhaps at a second home used for the hunting season, the staff packed up the house for long periods and enjoyed a little more time to themselves. In this instance, they were given an extra bonus to make up for the lack of dinner scraps, known as a 'board wage', to spend on food.

Coming from households where lack of money had meant a steady diet of bread and potatoes, the majority of the servants were better fed than they had ever been. Canterbury lad Frank Honey, employed as a houseboy while still at the local school, found the food a considerable perk in one house. 'The beauty of that job as far as I was concerned was that I had a jolly good breakfast,' he said. 'Prior to that I might have taken a piece of bread and butter to school with me when I went out, but I used to get eggs and bacon there – something I never got at home.'

Below is the list of beer allowances for servants at Leighton Hall, the Lancashire home of the wealthy furniture-making family the Gillows, as recorded on 17 June 1893.

1893 Beer Allowance for Staff at Meals Only	Pints
Butler	3
Coachman	3
Groom	3
Cook	2
Lady's Maid	2
First Housemaid	2
Second Housemaid	2
Laundry Maid	1
Kitchen Maid	2
Extra man	2
Total Allowance	22

1893 June 17: At present three servants do not take beer.

Extra Allowances of Beer

[For] sweeping kitchen and other chimneys 4 times a year and cleaning back – two men each	1
For cleaning [garden walkway] Ash Path once a year – each man	1
For cleaning house and washhouse cisterns once a year – two men each	1
General coal loading day when they work all day. Each man. At dinner	1
During rest of day	2
Man going to Lancaster on return if [he is] sober	1
Postman on Sunday bringing and taking back [post]bag	1
Man staying at home on Sunday morning if not a servant getting beer in house	1

Beer was weaker than today's pub brands and the quantities allowed were unlikely to result in inebriated servants. As there was no time to go to the pubs or clubs more than once a week, it was considered sensible to allow the servants to enjoy a pint with a meal and, for the upper staff, there would be wine as well.

PERKS AND EXTRAS

As well as the day-to-day sustenance, there were many perks to be had below stairs, especially for the more senior servants and those who waited on guests. For the lady's maids and valets they came in the form of gifts from the master and mistress and cast-off clothes that could be worn or sold on. Housemaids who were lucky enough to become temporary ladies' maids may also have received a financial boost for their trouble.

The footmen would pick up the odd shilling as a tip for attending to guests in the hallway or helping them into carriages and, while accompanying employers on a trip to a wealthier establishment, would be invited to participate in the fine cuisine in the kitchen.

Alfred West, a groom and valet for an old gentleman in the Edwardian era, remembered taking him on shooting and hunting trips to Hertfordshire, where he was allowed to taste his share of the spoils. 'The game was wonderful,' he said in *Lost Voices of the Edwardians*. 'I used to be treated very well. When I was working in the stables, washing down the horses after the hunt, I was able to go into the servants' quarters in the "Big House" and I was given the same food the toffs had had, after they'd finished with it. There was pheasant, duck and venison. It built me up no end.'

Being in charge of the wine cellar, the butler was expected to sample the goods before serving them at the table and one or two were known to overindulge from time to time. He may also have been given the occasional bottle as a perk for overseeing the cellar, the usual tariff being one bottle to every six opened, and was able to take the odd nip of the stronger tipples in his care, such as brandy and port. A shrewd butler could make a few bob selling candle ends, corks and the like and, in addition, visiting guests would also dig deep to cross his palm with silver.

Gratuities

A contemporary etiquette guide called *The Manners of Modern Society* examines the thorny subject of gratuities:

Servants, like railway porters, look after the douceurs [sweeteners]. All those who have rendered a guest any assistance look for acknowledgement and their hands are always on the alert when the moment of your departure arrives, to receive and close upon the gold or silver deposited therein.

A lady gives to the maid who has assisted with her toilette and the housemaid. A gentleman remembers the valet, the butler, coachman, gamekeeper – all or any who have rendered him any service.

Down in the basement, the extras depended on the opportunity and honesty of the staff. Cooks were given rabbit skins and offcuts to keep or sell and could raise a few shillings for the animal fats produced from roasting tins. Some sent a little of the food that arrived at the back door home to their families. Margaret Thomas remembers working with one cook who dispatched her with a parcel of groceries to send home each week, as soon as the orders arrived. 'As well she had commission from the tradesmen every month when the books were paid, and woe betide them if they didn't turn up with it, because there were complaints about their goods until they did. Because of these extras perhaps it didn't matter that the cook's wages were only £45 per year.'

The housekeeper, being in charge of daily expenditure, had plenty of opportunity to line her own pockets, honestly or otherwise. Like cook, she might receive a sweetener from the traders she used to provide linen, cleaning goods and food or even made money by showing interested tourists round the grand house. One fortunate lady, Mrs Hume, was housekeeper at Warwick Castle in the nineteenth century and, by showing interested visitors around the property, she managed to pile up a fortune of £30,000, now worth £1.3 million, in wages and gratuities.

ACCOMMODATION

In her 1905 children's novel *A Little Princess*, Frances Hodgson Burnett describes a servant's attic bedroom, from the point of view of a child used to a more privileged existence. Although a fictional room, it is undoubtedly similar to those found in almost any upper-class home:

Yes, this was another world. The room had a slanting roof and was whitewashed. The whitewash was dingy and had fallen off in places. There was a rusty grate, an old iron bedstead, and a hard bed covered with a faded coverlet. Some pieces of furniture too much worn to be used downstairs had been sent up. Under the skylight in the roof, which showed nothing but an oblong piece of dull grey sky, there stood an old battered red footstool.

Maids were invariably placed in the attic, partly because there were rooms there that the family didn't use and partly to keep them as far away as possible from the male staff, to deter 'fraternization'. For this reason the maids' corridor, often guarded by a formidable housekeeper or head housemaid, was known as the 'Virgin's wing'.

Bare Necessities

The basic furniture in the attic rooms varied little from house to house. There was a mattress on a small iron bedstead for each maid, a washstand with a jug for water, as very few had running water, and a basin, soap dish and toothbrush holder which rarely matched, having been passed down from the 'best bedrooms' when a companion piece had been broken. Some would have chairs and all would have bare floorboards, unlike the thick rugs and carpets of the family rooms. Servants' beds, which

Established in 1810, Heal's bed-making firm provided 'Simple Bedroom Furniture' suitable for a servant's room, as well as more luxury products

measured 2 ft 6 in. across rather than the usual single width of 3 ft, were sold in furniture shops and a junior maid would usually share her room, if not the same bed, with others. One scullery maid recalled sharing 'a bare-boarded room with the kitchen maid, quite separate from the other nine staff. A single iron bedstead with a lumpy mattress, a large chest of drawers and spotted glass, washstand, jug and basin and chamber pot. Considered to be well-furnished.'

Private Utilities

Ornaments and pictures were strictly forbidden in most servants' bedrooms and the attics were bitterly cold in the winter, with the poor incumbent usually waking to a frozen flannel and ice in the washing jug. Even when electricity and gas became common in society homes, employers trying to save on their budget usually left the attic out of the expensive installation. Similarly, while the dawning of the twentieth century saw an increasing trend towards fitted bathrooms with running water, the privilege rarely extended to the lowly staff. They usually took a tin bath in the room once a week on their afternoon off, or were allowed to bath in the wash house, using the water that had washed the linen.

One former maid said they had been banned from the family's two bathrooms. 'We had a tin bath in our bedroom which was in the attic and we had a lot of stairs to take our hot water up.' As they had no gas lamps in their rooms, they carried candles to bed with them at night. Dorothy Shaw, a tweeny in Newbury, told author Frank Dawes that she once asked her mistress for a candle to light her room, prompting the harsh lady to cut a candle in half with the comment, 'I don't encourage my servants to read in bed.'

Behind the Green Baize Door

In order that the frenzied activity of the servants didn't impinge on the peace and quiet of the household, there was a second staircase, unlit, between the attic where the maids lived and the basement where they worked. The servants' stairs were behind the aforementioned green baize door, and led to a network of tunnels and passages few from the other side would ever need to see. The servants' entrance was around the back of the house and, in town houses, was below ground level. It was considered a heinous impertinence for anyone of servant or tradesman class to call at the front door.

Along with the kitchen and scullery, the basement housed the sleeping quarters for the male members of staff as well as the butler's pantry and the housekeeper's room, where the preserves and pickles would be kept. If the housekeeper was lucky she would have enough room there to entertain one or two senior staff after supper, and share a glass of port. In large houses, the male staff slept in dormitory-style accommodation downstairs with lesser mortals, like the houseboy, bedding down on a fold-up cot in the servants' hall. As the butler's pantry was also home to the hugely valuable plates of gold and silver, and finest china, the butler, or perhaps a trusted footman, would sleep with his bed across the doorway.

For most domestics, conditions were undoubtedly an improvement on what they grew up with. The only difference at

---

Maid Simple

In retrospect Cynthia Asquith, a debutante in the Edwardian era, agreed that 'We are now shocked, and rightly so, by the poorness of the sleeping quarters into which our grandmothers' maids used to be packed, and such apparent disregard for their bodily comfort seems not only inconsiderate but short-sighted.' But, in *In Front of the Green Baize Door*, she argued that the substandard accommodation needed to be put in to the perspective of the day. The children of the house were, she claimed, 'very little better lodged than its staff. The plain fact was that at that time the standards of hygiene and comfort by which living conditions are judged today had not yet come into existence.'

---

home was that they didn't have to compare their own standard of living and social status with those who lived under the same roof.

The scant accommodation was not confined to the older buildings. Even in newly designed flats in London, servants' quarters were built that were condemned by medical magazine *The Lancet* in August 1905 for their lack of natural light. Despite having a sun-drenched reception room and two well-lit bedrooms the staff bedrooms in the new town dwellings were, it claimed, 'almost in darkness and but very imperfectly ventilated'. It went on to express concern that middle-class employers 'can allow themselves to take flats where they themselves are housed in comfort but where the servants live under conditions which, to say the least of them, must be eminently depressing'.

Even after the Second World War, the few staff left in service didn't see much improvement in sleeping or bathing arrangements. Gill Tripp remembered that her aunt's housemaid, who had been with the family for forty years, always slept in the basement.

> *Mina and Catherine, the cook, had bedrooms in the basement, where they lived and worked. We called it 'the area'. It had very big windows but a huge wall just outside so it can't have got a lot of light. Mina, at least, came upstairs but I'm sure Catherine never saw daylight.*
>
> *They both had to bath in a scullery, which must have been awful. The door didn't lock and they bathed in a big fixed tub which, when it wasn't in use, was covered by a thick, wooden lid with all the pots and pans stacked on top.*

Behind Closed Doors

Perhaps the best deal, in terms of accommodation, fell to the valets, ladies' maids and nursery nurses. The valet and the lady's maid usually had the great privilege of a bedroom adjoining that of the family member to which they attended and the nurse was given a bed in the night nursery, sleeping next to the children. In her autobiographical book *Small Talk*, Naomi Mitchison described the relationship with her nurse, Sina, 'whom I now remember as someone who was always nice to me, perhaps because "a servant" would never be allowed to punish me'. She suffered from bad dreams as a child and continues, 'Sina slept beside me. But sometimes she didn't wake and the nightmare went on in the dark, even though I seemed to be awake myself.'

The Servants' Hall

It wasn't only the employer and his family who lorded it over their social inferiors. The servants' hall, where the staff were served their meals, had strict rules of etiquette and a definite pecking order which meant the lower servants had to watch their Ps and Qs just as much downstairs as they did upstairs. Footman Frederick John Gorst, who worked for the extremely wealthy Duke of Portland at Welbeck Abbey, remembered the senior staff being referred to as the 'Upper Ten' – being the steward, the wine butler, the under-butler, the groom of chambers, the duke's valet, the housekeeper, head housemaid and ladies' maids. The lesser staff, which despite their considerable number were called the 'Lower Five', would not be allowed to eat with the 'Upper Ten', who took their meals in the Steward's Dining Room. They used fine china and linen napkins and were served with wine while the others had beer. The lower ranking servants aspired to join their 'betters' through internal promotion and this inspired hard work and good conduct.

In most grand houses the senior servants were known as 'Pugs' and the room which they reserved as their own was dubbed Pugs' Parlour. This could be a dining area where meals were taken away from the other staff or a sitting room where they took cheese, port and coffee after their meals. It was often the housekeeper's own parlour.

'There was a hallboy who waited on us in the servants' hall and on the housekeeper's room, which we called "Pugs' Parlour",' wrote Margaret Thomas. 'I was amused when I first saw the "Pugs' Parade". This happened after the first course: the butler, cook, ladies' maids and any visiting maids and valets, each took their glass of water in one hand and a piece of bread in the other, and proceeded out of the servants' hall down the passage to the housekeeper's room where their sweet was served. This departure was the signal for the first footman to carve us a second helping all round.'

At supper, Margaret remembered, the Pugs were served roast chicken and a dessert while the other staff were given one course of cold meat.

Outdoors Staff

A good head gardener was a valuable asset at the turn of the century. A breathtaking garden added to the prestige of the house and the aristocracy looked after their gardeners well. A cottage would be provided in the grounds and, as they were not expected to eat at the house, they were given an allowance for coal and milk, plus free vegetables from the garden. From 1903 until 1944, John Mcleod worked for the Marquess and Marchioness of Lothian at Monteviot, their estate on the Scottish Borders. He had twenty gardeners under him, a cottage, a fuel allowance and a starting salary of £65. His contract referred to fifty-five tons of coal annually, of which six was for Mcleod with the rest being used in the bothy and hothouses around the gardens. The estate even paid to put his children through grammar school. When he was offered a job working for the city of Glasgow in 1915, Lady Lothian doubled his wages to entice him to stay.

The grooms and coachmen would often be housed in rooms above the stables so that they could keep an eye on the horses and be constantly called upon by their masters. The head groom would earn around £40, and would have several grooms under him, but as motor cars became more and more fashionable in the early part of the twentieth century, numbers dwindled and the head groom gave way to chauffeur-mechanics. Former groom Henry Lansley recalled in *Lost Voices of the Edwardians* being sent to London to learn to drive in 1910: 'The first car I drove was a new 16 hp Wolseley. My employer had taken a hunting box in Warwickshire. On my way a terrific snowstorm set in and, as there were no windscreen wipers, I couldn't see a thing. So I stopped in Rugby for the night and went on next day.' The car also had no spare wheel. 'Only the rear wheels were braked, and as there was no self-starters, it was always necessary to swing the handle at the front.'

UNIFORM

Maids

In order to go into service, a maid had to have her own uniform of a print dress, a black dress and several white aprons. Coming from extremely poor backgrounds, as well as workhouses and orphanages, saving up for these garments was no mean feat and most would have to work in part-time jobs for two years to make the money. A black dress alone would cost around 15s. (75p), the equivalent of £43 in today's money, and the entire wardrobe could come to over £4 (£229 today), which was a fortune to a young girl hoping to go into service.

At fourteen, Margaret Thomas was told she must stop helping her mother around the house and find a job to buy 'clothes for service'. She started by looking after a baby, from early morning until late at night, for which she was paid a weekly wage of 2s., the equivalent of £5.70 today. Her employer let rooms and, when no rent was coming in, Margaret's pay was reduced to 1s. 6d.

A housemaid wearing a typical uniform of the time

'I couldn't save much out of my wages so when they dropped I got another job as well,' she said. 'I was paid one-and-six a week to clean boots and knives from 7.30 a.m. to 9.30 a.m. before I went to my other place.' Eventually she saved enough to buy the outfits she needed – print dresses, aprons, black dress, stiff collars and cuffs, all packed into the small tin trunk which was the only luggage a new maid was permitted.

Print dresses and 'morning aprons' of coarse hessian were worn for the filthy menial work that filled the early hours of the day, such as cleaning grates, scrubbing floors and laying fires. At lunchtime, maids changed into the smarter attire of black dresses and starched white 'afternoon aprons' so that they would be suitably dressed to lay tables and serve lunch, even if

---

Dorothy Green

Londoner Dorothy came from an orphanage and was put out to work at the age of eleven to save for her uniform: 'I went to work at a local house for a few hours each day, scrubbing floors, sweeping up and cleaning the range. They weren't grand enough to have a proper maid so they paid me two shillings a week and I wore my own clothes. It took two years to buy the material and sew my first cotton dress and aprons for service, and buy the plain black costume, but I was glad when I had because it meant I could get a position in a good house.'

---

it was only in the servants' hall. The aprons covered both skirt and bust, with white straps over the shoulders that criss-crossed on the back. White cotton mobcaps were also worn, often with lace or ribbon streamers flowing down the back.

The maids' white aprons and cuffs were expected to be absolutely pristine at all times, and hours were spent starching and pressing them. They were all hand sewn and one pattern from 1909 suggested that a maid's apron was the perfect gift for any family with a girl who may go into service.

'Many ladies interest themselves in procuring good situations for young girls going out to service, and these know how important it is that the girls should be properly outfitted with all things necessary to keep them neat and tidy,' it read. 'This outfit is often a matter of some difficulty in a large and poor family, and a few gifts of useful garments are an immense boon. Strong aprons are easy things to make, and any young servant would gratefully receive a present of four of these. The pattern given is suitable for a young woman of sixteen or seventeen, and the cost of making is as follows:

1¾ yards of apron linen, 36 inches wide, at 8*d*.	1*s*. 2*d*.
Linen buttons and sewing cotton	0*s*. 2*d*.
Total Cost	1*s*. 4*d*.

In the houses that could not afford the more expensive front-of-house staff, such as a butler and footmen, the maids' appearance was of the utmost importance. In *Manchester Made Them* Katherine Campbell Chorley described the upper-middle-class street where she was raised in Alderley Edge, Cheshire. Her father was a wealthy businessman and their similarly prosperous neighbours competed over the issue of servants, who were treated as a status symbol.

'There were no butlers but the maids were excessively trim, clad in starched print of a morning and in black and brown with finely woven aprons in the afternoon and always, of course, wearing a cap as a badge of office.'

She added, 'The trimmer the maid and the more distant her manner the more intimidating the formality of one's entrance.'

Specialist shops in the town centres sold the material and clothing for servants and these were situated away from the highbrow fashion houses frequented by their employers. Katherine recalled one lunch visit at a middle-class home when she made something of a faux pas.

'The conversation was on shopping and the various smart and expensive shops in Manchester were being reviewed. Suddenly I burst out that I thought all these shops were nonsense.

'"Oldham Street is much the best place to shop," I announced didactically.

'Now only those who know the social nuances of Manchester in the first decade of the century can understand the enormity of this remark. For Oldham Street was where the maids made their purchases and you did not invade their preserves. It was like going to church on Sunday evening or visiting your doctor during his consulting hours instead of having him attend you. There was a chilly silence and I felt that perhaps I had gone too far.'

By the Edwardian era it had become standard practice for mistresses to give their maids a Christmas present of a length of cloth which would have to be made into a new uniform at the girl's own expense. If the maid was not able to sew the costume herself, either through lack of ability or time, it might cost her three or four precious shillings to have 'made up', an expense many resented.

Underneath all the starched uniforms the maids, even in the Edwardian era, were expected to wear corsets, which would have made their domestic work much more difficult. It can't have been easy scrubbing floors in such restricting undergarments. The rest of their underwear was calico or flannelette, as silk underwear, a favourite of the debutantes, was widely regarded as sinful among the servant classes. The maids also had to provide their own stockings, which cost around 4d. and would be darned until they could no longer be worn.

Cassell's Household Guide commented, 'Dress in these days is a very disputed point between mistress and maid. Any attempt to restrict young women in the choice of their garments will be found fruitless. Certain fashions, however, which are likely to be destructive to the employer's property, or unfitted for the performance of a servant's duties, a lady has a right to prohibit [...] If ladies would be at a little pains to mention their wishes on this subject, young women in service would supply themselves with suitable wardrobes. Whatever clothing a servant chooses to wear when out for a holiday is beyond a mistress's rule.'

In the nursery, the nanny wore a white or grey cotton print dress and apron and, when out walking with the children, was permitted a black, navy or dark plum coat and a black straw bonnet.

Lillian's Story

At the age of fifteen, in 1908, Lillian Westall started in domestic service in the middle-class home of a clerk and his wife, who had two children. She was a nurse and housemaid and received 2s. a week.

In the morning I did the housework: in the afternoon I took the children out: in the evening I looked after them and put them to bed. My employers didn't seem to have much money themselves but they liked the idea of having 'a nursemaid' and made me buy a cap, collar, cuffs and apron. Then the mistress took me to have a photograph taken with the children grouped around me.

Professor John Burnett, *Useful Toil*

Senior Staff

The lady's maid, like the housekeeper, was allowed to wear her own clothes but, while the latter was likely to opt for a sober black or grey dress, which would emphasize the required no-nonsense approach and give an air of gravitas, the former was likely to be inclined towards 'fripperies'. Although it was her job to be interested in the latest styles and fabrics, it would not do for the maid to get ideas above her station. She might have been given her mistress's unwanted dresses but a late Victorian publication was scandalized by these 'abigails disguised as their betters'. For example, if a lady's maid indulged in black silk stockings, instead of the usual grey, she may well have incurred the wrath of her mistress.

The lady's maid rarely wore the starched apron and cap considered the badge of servitude by the lower servants, but she occasionally wore a tiny, decorative apron when washing her mistress's hair. Being an expert needlewoman was an essential qualification, which also proved helpful when she was altering her employer's cast-offs in order to wear them herself.

The Butler

This distinguished figure wore a black suit styled to the fashion of the day, with a waistcoat and watchchain and a black tie.

In the evening, when serving in the dining room, he changed to tails, worn with a black tie as opposed to the white tie customarily worn by the master and his male guests.

'I've always found it interesting that when the butler serves food to the family and guests at night he puts on his tails, and is actually wearing the same outfit as the guests,' commented *Downton Abbey* creator Julian Fellowes.

The Footmen

As they were the living representation of a family's wealth, the fine livery of these ornamental workers made them the peacocks of the domestic world. They were presented with tailored jackets, waistcoats, knee breeches and smart white shirts. They were expected to look dapper at all times and particular attention was paid to their hair, which had to be neatly combed and powdered with flour of violet powder, which then had to be washed out in the evening.

Margaret Thomas first saw a footman in full livery when she went for an interview for a job in a Yorkshire household in the early 1900s: 'I remember a powdered footman was taking an airing on the area steps next door,' she said. 'He looked very grand with his scarlet breeches but he was the only one I ever saw, they were disappearing then.'

It was a bone of contention among the female staff that, while the lowliest maid had to scrimp and save to buy her own uniform, the footman, who earned a higher annual wage than the majority of the female staff, was provided with his.

Mrs Beeton advised mistresses that 'The footman only finds himself in stockings, shoes, and washing. Where silk stockings, or other extra articles of linen are worn, they are found by the family, as well as his livery, a working dress, consisting of a pair of overalls, a waistcoat, a fustian jacket, with a white or jean one for times when he is liable to be called to answer the door or wait at breakfast; and, on quitting his service, he is expected to leave behind him any livery had within six months.'

In the most well-to-do households the footman would have a daytime livery and an evening livery, and a great deal of time was spent changing uniforms and seeing to his elaborate hairstyle with soap and powder.

Young boys taken on as footmen were referred to as 'tigers' due to the striped outfit. Their job was often to ride on the coaches and jump down to hold the horse's head when the master wished to stop, although they were put to work in many other ways. The Victorian Prime Minister Lord Salisbury, for example, used to enjoy whizzing down the steep slopes of Hatfield House on a tricycle. He would take a 'tiger' with him to push it up who would then be obliged to jump on the back as his eminent master set off downhill.

The vast cost of the livery, along with the popularity of cars and the rising cost of employing male staff, was one of the reasons that the position of footman became increasingly

The footman in his livery

rare in Edwardian Britain. The few footmen that remained in the grander houses became even more impressive as a badge of wealth.

CHAPTER FOUR

A Day in the Life of a Country House

THE WORKING DAY was an incredibly long one for Edwardian servants; they were on the go from dawn until bedtime. The house needed to be cleaned and the fires lit before the family rose and most were unable to retire until the master and mistress were in bed, or had instructed them they were no longer needed.

'These people *worked* from the moment they got up in the morning until they went to bed at night,' explains *Downton Abbey* consultant Alastair Bruce. 'Underlining that there wasn't really time off in the way that we expect today. There is constant activity. It's quite a juxtaposition, the frantic activity downstairs, delivering the calm, peace, serenity of the family who are living in the house.'

Each house ran to a different timetable and Margaret Thomas remembered one Yorkshire home where the second housemaid 'had to be downstairs at 4 a.m. every morning to get the sitting room done before breakfast. The second housemaid had a medal room to keep clean, where the medals were set out in steel cases, and had to be polished with emery paper every day.'

Cynthia Asquith recalled life from the other side of the green baize door. 'In some really well-ordered households it was even the rule that no maid should ever be seen broom or duster in hand. Except for the bedrooms all the housework had to be done before any of the family or their guests came downstairs, a refinement that meant very early rising for the maids.'

Although the length of the day varied, most larger houses were up and running by 6 a.m. The busiest part of the day for the maids was the morning, while the footmen came into their own in the afternoon and the cooks were kept busy right up until dinner. Even when the maids were supposed to be having a short break in the afternoon, they were constantly at the mercy of the servant bells. These common devices were operated by a pull or switch in each room, which triggered a bell that sounded in the basement. Downstairs, the bells were mounted on a panel signalling which room it had been rung from, thereby indicating the location of the family member or guest requiring some assistance. The resting footman or maid would then leap to his or her feet and rush up the stairs to find out what was needed. In her memoirs *Below Stairs* Margaret Powell remembered the servants' bells located in the passage outside the kitchen in her first job as a maid, when she was fourteen.

In this passage, hanging on the wall, was a long row of bells with indicators above them to show where they rang from, and it was my job every time a bell rang to run full tilt out to the passage to see which bell it was [...] If you didn't run like mad out to the passage, the bell would stop ringing before you got there and you had no idea whether it was from the blue room, the pink room, first bedroom, second bedroom, fifth bedroom, drawing room or dining room. I was always in trouble over those bells at first, but at last I mastered the art, and nobody shot out quicker than me when they rang.

Which room to rush to?

A TYPICAL DAY

6 a.m.: Scullery maids and kitchen maids are first up to light the kitchen range and heat the water needed for washing. They also boil water for tea and scrub the kitchen floor. The hallboy is also beginning his working day by polishing boots and making sure there is enough chopped wood and coal for all the fires in the house.

6.30 a.m.: The kitchen maid makes tea and toast for the housekeeper and ladies' maids. Taking them up to their rooms is the job of the housemaids, who have just risen and dressed before coming down to the kitchen to fetch the trays. The butler opens the shutters and unlocks all the doors in preparation for the day ahead. Having attended the seniors, the housemaids set about cleaning and blacking the hearths and setting the fires in the downstairs rooms.

7 a.m.: The scullery maid makes sure all the washing-up from the night before is finished and put away while the kitchen maid cooks breakfast for the staff and takes tea to the cook. The housemaids are busy dusting and sweeping in the downstairs rooms, in

order to have them spotless by the time the family appear. The maid-of-all-work or 'between-stairs maid' scrubs the front step and polishes the brass knocker on the front door.

7.30 a.m.: The cook takes food deliveries and the gardener comes to the back door with the day's vegetables and any fruit that is in season in the grounds. Cook then begins preparing breakfast for the family. The nursery maid takes breakfast for the nurse and the young children up to the nursery. The chambermaids take tea trays and hot water for washing and shaving to the rooms of the family and any guests that are staying and light the bedroom fires. They also remove and empty chamber pots from each room. The hallboy sets the table for the servants' breakfast.

8 a.m.: Breakfast is served in the servants' hall. The lady's maid finishes her breakfast before seeing to the mistress's bath. The butler or valet takes a bowl of hot water to his master's bedroom for the morning shave. The footmen lay the table for the family breakfast.

8.30a.m: For all those able to attend, prayers or mass are held in the chapel or, if none, the library or parlour. For many of the downstairs staff this is the only time they will see the family. For some, however, it was hard to concentrate on their godly pursuit. 'What a farce those prayers were for me,' commented former kitchen maid Margaret Thomas, 'for I worried all the time in case my fire had got low, as I had the toast to make the moment I got out.' Announcements to staff, and the occasional scolding, would be given out during this time.

9 a.m.:   The family breakfast is served. While the servants have had porridge or, if they are lucky, bacon and eggs, their employers will be greeted with an array of silver covered dishes with bacon, eggs, kippers, kedgeree, devilled kidneys, freshly baked rolls and fruit.

9.30 a.m.:   After clearing the plates and cleaning the tables the housemaids or parlourmaids turn their attention to the laundry as the scullery maid washes up. The chambermaids are busy cleaning the bedrooms and one of the footmen is on duty at the front door, in case of callers. The butler decants the wine.

10 a.m.:   The butler has a morning meeting in his master's study to go through the business of the day. At the same time the cook is meeting with the lady of the house to present menus, find out who will be attending each meal and receive details of any guests for dinner.

10.30 a.m.: As the rest of the domestic staff go about their usual chores, the kitchen maid and the cook are in the kitchen, preparing luncheon. The maid chops vegetables, weighs ingredients and crushes herbs before getting the servants' simple lunch underway. In the butler's pantry, the second footman is polishing the cutlery as the hallboy sharpens knives.

11 a.m.:   Servants gather for a morning tea break and are issued with orders for the rest of the day. The footmen are then dispatched to lay the table for luncheon.

12 p.m.:   The servants' meal is served. Although the family's midday meal is known as luncheon, the domestic staff sit down to 'dinner' at noon. Servants were better fed than their working-class counterparts and had a reasonably balanced diet. Lunch is also served in the nursery at the same time.

1 p.m.:   Lunch is served to the family by the butler. If no family member is out, a footman may be available to help serve. The three-course meal may include a joint of meat that is always carved by the butler. Any leftovers will go towards the servants' next meal.

2 p.m.:   The table is cleared once more and the washing-up started in the butler's pantry by the hallboy. The scullery maid washes the servants' dishes in the scullery. The footmen will now accompany the lady of the house on her visits and the master of the house on any business meetings.

2.30 p.m.: The cook is baking scones, muffins and rolls for tea while the maids have a break, providing all their work is done.

3 p.m.:   The lady's maid is summoned to help the mistress into her tea gown, if she has returned from her calls.

4 p.m.:   Tea is served to the family. A selection of sandwiches, scones, muffins and cakes will be taken in the drawing room or, in good weather, on the lawn. The kitchen maid is busy preparing the vegetables for the evening meal and rustling up the servants' tea.

The Tea Table, as illustrated in
Mrs Beeton's Book of Household Management

5.30 p.m.:   All the servants enjoy a light meal.

6 p.m.:   The basement kitchen is now in full swing, as the five-course meal is prepared. The main course, which often follows a fresh fish course, will be meat with a selection of vegetables. If guests are staying the meal may be further extended, with seven or eight courses quite customary. The scullery maid is washing pots as they are used and the footmen are once more setting the table. The butler will check the plates and the silver, to make sure they are clean, polish the wine glasses and cast a critical eye over the cutlery. He is also in charge of the salads and desserts

that are prepared in his pantry. The footmen lay the table, once more, for the sumptuous feast ahead.

7 p.m.: The ladies of the household retire to their chambers to bathe in water scented with bath salts and dress for dinner and their maids join them to help. The dinner gowns are still worn over corsets and button up at the back so their attendants needs to be on hand to fasten them, as well as to wash and restyle hair. If there is a valet in the house he will attend to the master. Guests' own valets and ladies' maids were often on hand to attend to their own employers.

8 p.m.: Dinner is served in the dining room. The first course is already on the table as the footmen are on hand to pull chairs out as the diners are seated. The butler will pour the wine and then stand motionless at the sideboard through each course, recharging the glasses only when signalled by the master of the house.

9 p.m.: With the last course prepared and ready to go out to the table, the kitchen staff and maids sit down to supper. The serving staff will only be allowed to rest when the final course is eaten.

9.30 p.m.:   The footmen clear the plates while the kitchen maids and hallboy begin the washing-up.

10 p.m.:   Upstairs, the ladies take coffee in the dining room while the men retire to the smoking room for port and masculine conversation. The butler needs to be on duty in case he is required and the below-stairs staff are unable to go to bed until the word comes down that no more refreshments are needed.

10.30 p.m.: The cook and the housekeeper may retire, having checked that all is in order in the basement, but the scullery maid and kitchen maid are still busy with their final chores, blacking the kitchen range, cleaning the flues and sweeping the stone floors. The hallboy ends his day by filling the coalscuttles and stocking up on chopped wood in preparation for the fires in the morning, and cleaning the shoes and boots which the family and guests have left outside their bedroom doors.

11 p.m.:   The butler locks all the outer doors and any open shutters and makes sure the fires have died down safely before going to bed.

Being the last to be relieved of his duties, the butler had the longest day and, should his master have been a night owl, he might not have got to bed until the early hours. According to records at Leighton Hall, in Lancashire, the butler there was up and ready for work by 6.45 a.m. and expected to be on hand to lock up at 1 a.m. Notes issued by the head of the household Mr Richard Gillow, in 1893, outlined the butler's timetable.

Butler's Duties	
Calling Mr & Mrs Gillow	6.45
Take tea to Mr Gillow and take key of Hall door	7.30
Breakfast in storeroom	8.00
Attend mass if any or morning prayers	9.00
Parlour Breakfast	9.30
Servants' Dinner	12.00
Parlour Luncheon	1.15
Tea in Drawing Room	5.00
Dinner	7.00
Servants' supper	8.15
Night Prayers	9.15
Tea in Drawing Room	9.30
Lock up and Bed	1.00

His instructions detailed the areas he had to lock up as 'two outside passage doors downstairs, Servants' hall, Shoe place and Pantries. Lock door and window of Centre Room, Dining Room, Front Hall and Morning Room if occupied by the family who keep the keys at night.'

HIGH DAYS AND HOLIDAYS

In the Victorian household most servants were given just one afternoon off a week, on Sunday, so that they could attend church. In addition, if the mistress was a benevolent one, they might have had an extra day off a month.

Cassell's Household Guide suggested the generous extra day did away with the necessity for a maid's friends to call on her at the house. 'At the same time, a mistress should be careful not to bind herself to spare her servant on a certain day in every month, as is sometimes demanded,' it advised. '"Once in a month when convenient" is a better understanding. Most servants, in addition to the monthly holiday, ask to be allowed to go to church of a Sunday once in the day. This request is reasonable; and if a servant really goes to a place of worship, some inconvenience should be borne by her employers to secure her this liberty, but if she goes instead to see her friends, it should be a matter for consideration whether she shall go out or not. At any rate, the absence ought not to extend very much beyond the time occupied in the church service.'

With sixteen-hour days standard for a hard-working maid, an extra day was a remarkably small concession and, with so many working away from home, it could be months or even years between visits to see their families and friends 'back home'. Frank Dawes writes of one homesick teenage maid, Harriet Brown, who wrote to her mother in 1870: 'Dear Mother, I should of ask you over next week only we are going to have two dinner parties one on Tuesday the other on Thursday and we shall be so busy so you must come after it is over [...] I should so like to see you but I cannot get away just now so you must come and see me soon.' Although this was thirty years before the Edwardian age, little changed in that time and even Harriet's own daughter was to go into service as a child twenty years after her mother.

By 1900, calls for fairer working conditions had led to an afternoon and an evening off each week, as well as church time on Sunday. But the free time was not enshrined in law and only began after lunchtime duties were completed, often as late as 3 p.m. There would also be a curfew, usually around 9 p.m., and anyone late back could find himself or herself locked out by the angry housekeeper. Time off could also be cruelly snatched away for the smallest misdemeanour or the overlooking of a task.

Dorothy Green was the youngest maid in a London home in the early 1900s and often had to wait up to let her colleagues in after a night out. 'The younger ones had to be back by

GOING OUT. Usually one night a week and the alternate Sunday afternoon and evening are given ; in some places one day a month is also given. The yearly holiday naturally depends on varying circumstances, but it usually extends from a week to a fortnight.

Most women-servants are allowed 1/- weekly for laundry expenses, it being supposed that they will get up their own smaller things, such as collars, cuffs, caps, etc. For nurse-maids 2/- to 2/6, and for men-servants 1/6 per week is usual.

Advice on the provision of a servant's days off, from the Manual of Household Work and Management *by Annie Butterworth (1913)*

8 p.m. and the older ones at 9 p.m. If the maids were late, which they frequently were, I would be trembling with fear in the kitchen and hoping the mistress didn't decide to check up on them because I knew there would be an almighty row if she found out.'

As the work was relentless and exhausting, there was little time to rest or play so the afternoons or evenings off were highly treasured. But not everyone had the energy left to enjoy them to the full. Margaret Thomas reflected on one house where she was given alternate Sunday afternoons and evenings off. 'Sometimes, when I went up to dress, I was too tired to go out so I lit the gas fire and thought I'd have a short rest. I was vexed when much later the cook coming up to bed found me there and discovered I'd "had" my day out.'

For those who did get a monthly day off, it was a much-anticipated chance for a family reunion. Girls frequently started in service as young as twelve and would miss their parents and siblings terribly, so their monthly visit was a cause for celebration and a chance to push the boat out. A kind cook would send each girl home with treats such as preserves, cold meats and cakes and, after church, the gathered family would enjoy a tasty spread perhaps topped off with some home-grown musical entertainment.

For those in service in a London house, with family living in the city, a journey on a tram, a bus or the 'tuppenny tube' would get them home. For those living further away, the journey was difficult and expensive, especially on a maid's wage. Although the Cheap Trains Act of 1883 had removed duty from all journeys charged at less than a penny a mile, this applied mostly to 'workmen's trains' in city and suburban areas. A longer journey, even in second class, would mean a lot of saving had to be done first. For example, a trip from London to Dover, would take two-and-a-half hours and cost over 6s. (30p), a great deal of money for someone earning £16 a year. The cost, and the fact that servants were often expected to return before late dinner was served, even on their one day off, made long distance visits to families impossible.

Enlightened employers, such as one family who engaged Margaret Thomas as a housemaid, allowed an overnight stay away, to combat this problem. In Margaret's case they also allowed her to save up her days off over a few months so she could pay a longer visit home.

At the beginning of the twentieth century, it became standard practice to allow a week's paid holiday, usually while the family was away itself. The lower paid staff would save up all year so that they could afford the train fare home for this precious week and a few small gifts for their parents and siblings. After the First World War, when domestic staff were demanding fairer pay and conditions, the holiday entitlement rose to two weeks.

CHURCH OUTINGS

Servants were expected to attend a church service on Sunday and anyone refusing would risk being branded 'wicked' in the pious era of Queen Victoria. Indeed, whenever they were in Balmoral, the monarch and her husband Prince Albert insisted their servants accompany them on the mile-and-a-half walk to Crathie church every Sunday, without fail.

Under her son, Edward VII, weekends in the upper echelons tended more to parties, horse racing and the pursuit of fun but mistresses still insisted on chapel attendance for their children and servants and most middle-class families were regular members of the congregation. A God-fearing staff was an obedient one and religion was not only thought good for the servants' souls but a convenient way of keeping them in check.

In some churches the master's family attended the morning service while the domestics worshipped at evening mass but in most the household attended together. However, they sat in

Sunday Best

Each maid had her Sunday best for church but, unlike the ladies that she waited on, this was not an occasion for flamboyant style statements. Staff were often instructed on exactly what they should wear and, even if the guidelines were general, they were invariably pressed to wear plain dark colours, with a dark coat and black shoes. A modest hat or bonnet was also worn as women would never attend church bareheaded.

different areas of the church, with the family settling themselves in a pew reserved each week for the residents of the 'big house' and servants relegated to the back or the gallery. Here, as in the servants' dining hall, the downstairs hierarchy was regimentally observed, with each servant seated according to their rank.

'All we maidservants [...] had to wear black, navy or dark grey whenever we went out, with small black hats or toques,' recalled Margaret Thomas. 'We had our own places in our pews at church, and I was agreeably surprised to find I ranked next to the head housemaid.'

In addition, daily prayers were read at home and the servants' areas were dotted with framed quotes, often embroidered, from the scriptures, extolling the virtues of hard work and cleanliness and reminding them of their righteous toil.

ENTERTAINMENT

On the rare occasions that servants could grab a few hours off, most, if close enough, would spend the day visiting family, seeing friends or meeting boyfriends and girlfriends. Those in service far from home would have had no time to make friends outside of their own colleagues and little money to spend on entertainment. But the options varied considerably depending on the area in which you lived.

Country Life

In country houses, the hours might be whiled away taking a healthy walk and getting the fresh air that those confined to the basement were so deprived of. If they were lucky, servants might be able to afford to spend their pennies taking tea in a local teashop savouring, no doubt, the experience of being waited on for once.

City Sights

In London, however, there were many choices for one's day off. Cinema, although in its infancy, was becoming a popular craze in the first decade of the twentieth century and a short film, depicting a news event or just an everyday scene of factory workers, was still a marvel. While there were picture shows at a couple of theatres in the capital, makeshift cinemas were also springing up in empty shops furnished with folding seats. The novelty was still huge and the public flocked to pay a penny and see their first flick.

An alternative was the music hall, still a hugely popular form of entertainment before the First World War. 'I went to the Bricks Music Hall and nearly fell over the front, right up in the gallery trying to look over, because it's very high,' said Albert Packman in *Lost Voices of the Edwardians*. 'There were acrobats on the stage and impossible things that I'd never thought of in all my life – all for tuppence.'

Leading acts included Marie Lloyd, who popularized such tunes as 'A Little Bit of What You Fancy Does You Good' and 'Where Did You Get That Hat?' and, a little later, Florrie Ford. A seat in the 'gods' could come in at sixpence, a hefty price for a lowly maid but reasonable enough for a young man in employment, should he wish to woo her.

A stroll 'up west' might be rewarded with a glimpse of royalty as they left Buckingham Palace and a few curiosities too. Mildred Ramson remembered an old lady who stood with her cow in St James's Park, every day, selling milk and cakes to passers-by. 'Another sight was Mr Leopold de Rothschild driving his tandem of zebras in the park,' she recalled. 'We used to admire, but not touch, the famous Piccadilly goat; we bowed as the old Queen, now deeply beloved, drove slowly by, or the Princess of Wales passed with her three daughters

Marie Lloyd, a leading act in Music Hall

packed in the back of a landau. Royalty passed with a stately step then.'

The footmen and grooms, if not of a mind to take a lady out for the evening, were likely to be found at the local pub.

CHAPTER FIVE

Toil and Technique

URING THE TWENTIETH century, domestic appliances became an integral part of everyday life and few modern-day homeowners could cope without their washing machine, vacuum cleaner or fridge. But the Edwardian servant had none of these luxuries to help them with their endless chores. Indeed, it was the very absence of labour-saving devices that kept so many of them in a job as even the average middle-class wife couldn't manage all the housework without some assistance.

Homes were beginning to be wired for electricity in the pre-war period but the expense of the wiring, and a deep-seated suspicion of any 'newfangled' inventions, meant that the majority of houses remained without mains power until after the First World War. Electric washing machines became available for homes in 1917 and fridges a year later but, again, only the wealthiest families could afford them. Similarly, gas cookers had been commercially available since the 1850s, but few mistresses bothered to have them installed and there was little or no access to mains gas outside major towns or cities.

As a consequence, everything had to be done by hand using traditional methods passed down through the generations and a lot of elbow grease. Stone floors were scrubbed with soap and water and to clean the carpets the parlourmaid would scatter damp tea leaves and then sweep them up, usually on her hands and knees.

One of the hardest tasks was cleaning and blacking the large kitchen range first thing in the morning before setting the fire. This was done with a block of black lead that could be bought for around 4*d*. (1.7p). The maid broke a little off each day and mixed it with water before applying with a brush.

An advertisement for Chivers' Carpet Soap in 1910,
a cleaning product designed to ease labour

Mrs Beeton sets out specific instructions for this arduous task, recommending the housemaid or kitchen maid should, 'lay a cloth (generally made of coarse wrapping) over the carpet in front of the stove, and on this should place her housemaid's box, containing black-lead brushes, leathers, emery-paper, cloth, black lead, and all utensils necessary for cleaning a grate, with the cinder-pail on the other side.

'She now sweeps up the ashes, and deposits them in her cinder-pail, which is a japanned tin pail, with a wire-sifter inside, and a closely fitting top. In this pail the cinders are sifted, and reserved for use in the kitchen or under the copper, the ashes only being thrown away. The cinders disposed of, she

---

Brunswick Black

One householders' bible includes a recipe for 'Brunswick black', which provided an 'excellent varnish' and would prove easier to clean:

INGREDIENTS – 1 lb of common asphaltum, ½ pint of linseed oil, 1 quart of oil of turpentine.
Mode – Melt the asphaltum, and add gradually to it the other two ingredients. Apply this with a small painter's brush, and leave it to become perfectly dry. The grate will need no other cleaning, but will merely require dusting every day, and occasionally brushing with a dry black-lead brush. This is, of course, when no fires are used. When they are required, the bars, cheeks, and back of the grate will need black-leading in the usual manner.

proceeds to black-lead the grate, producing the black lead, the soft brush for laying it on, her blacking and polishing brushes, from the box which contains her tools.'

With so many mouths to feed, on such a frequent basis, cook used an array of huge metal pots that were constantly being washed up by the kitchen maid or scullery maid and the cleaning products had to be mixed together from various household substances. Margaret Thomas recalled a sideboard

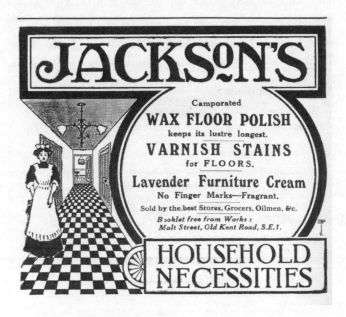

An advertisement for Jackson's Household Necessities from
Mrs Beeton's Family Cookery

display of huge copper pans that had to be cleaned until they sparkled, for the mistress's morning inspection, using a mixture of sand, salt, flour and vinegar, rubbed onto the metal by hand.

Beeswax and turpentine were used for polishing the floor and furniture polish could be made with equal proportions of linseed oil, turpentine, vinegar and wine.

THE SERVANT PROBLEM

The reluctance to provide labour-saving devices was typical of many employers' attitude towards their servants' toil and became a source of resentment in the early twentieth century, when other job opportunities were opening up for young women and servants were becoming increasingly hard to find. A 1944 report by the National Conference of Labour Women pointed out that this lack of consideration continued well after the First World War, when fewer and fewer women were going into service: 'Labour-saving equipment, which could easily have been afforded, was often not bought on the ground that unnecessary drudgery did not matter in the case of the servants.' But in the early 1900s, *The Sphere* magazine came down squarely on the side of the mistresses who wrung their unsullied hands as they despaired over the 'servant problem'. 'The servant who takes an interest in her work seems no longer to exist, and in return for high wages we get but superficial service,' bemoaned one editorial. 'Where is the maid to be found who takes pride in the brilliance of the glass to be used on the table or remembers of her own initiative to darn the damask? Every sort of contrivance now lessens labour – carpet sweepers, knife machines, bathrooms, lifts – in spite of these the life of a housewife is one long wrestle and failure to establish order.'

The Champion carpet sweeper was one concession which some of the progressive mistresses afforded their staff after its introduction in the 1870s. From 1905, it began to be replaced by the early vacuum cleaner, which used bellows to suck up the dust and was so cumbersome it would often take two maids

An advertisement from the early 1900s for a motorized
vacuum cleaner, designed by Hubert Cecil Booth

to operate it. One London girl, whose memories are stored at the Imperial War Museum, had to present her mistress with the dirt she had collected each time she vacuumed so that it could be weighed. She soon learned to save the old dirt to add to the collection, in order to impress the stringent lady: 'In the pothouse I had one or two bags of different colour with dirt in so I could make my weight up. What was the weight she wanted? About a cup and a half of dirt for each room.'

WASHDAY

In most houses washday fell on a Monday but laundry work went on all week. The traditional song 'Dashing Away with the Smoothing Iron' is the perfect illustration of the work involved in the weekly wash, as the object of the singer's affections is seen doing a different task every day of the week. Beginning on a Monday morning, when he catches her 'A-washing of her linen', the ditty has her hanging out on Tuesday, starching on Wednesday, ironing on Thursday, folding on Friday, airing on Saturday and finally wearing her finest linen on Sunday. This was no exaggeration as in a grand house there was enough work to keep a laundry maid busy all week. Here is her weekly timetable:

Monday

Mrs Beeton instructed that the laundry maid should begin on Monday morning by examining all the articles in her care and entering them into a log, known as the 'washing book'. Collars and cuffs were detached from clothing and then the washing sorted into five piles, depending on fabric. They were then placed in tubs of lukewarm water and lye soap and left to soak overnight.

Tuesday

The following day would find the maid with her arms immersed in a huge copper bath of hot water and soda crystals or 'yellow soap', rubbing and scrubbing to get all the marks out of the clothes, sheets and tablecloths. Whites would be bleached with lemon juice or, in some cases, urine, although this practice was dying out in the twentieth century. The items would then be rinsed and examined inch by inch for any stains that had survived the wash. These would then be tackled with a variety of traditional stain removers, including chalk for grease and oil, alcohol for grass stains, kerosene for bloodstains and hot coals wrapped in cloth for wax. Lemon juice and onion were used to lighten stains and, in order to whiten scorched linen, Mrs Beeton suggested a paste made from vinegar, fuller's earth, soap, onion juice and dried fowls' dung!

Wednesday

If possible sheets were hung outside to dry and bleach in the sunlight. If not, they would be hung in the drying room. More delicate items that could not be soaked, such as coloured silks and muslins, were washed separately with widely available yellow soap. Borax was often added to the water to prevent fading. They were then hung on a clotheshorse in the drying room, away from harmful rays of the sun. Woollen garments were washed in cold water, to prevent shrinkage. The copper pots then had to be cleaned, the York stone floor of the wash house scrubbed and everything put back in its correct place.

Thursday and Friday

The laundry maid's week would end with the starching, mangling and ironing. Household items such as tablecloths, aprons, collars, shirtfronts and cuffs would need to be stiffened to avoid wrinkles and, to do this, they were dipped in a paste made from starch and water. The actual starch could be bought but home-made varieties made from potato, rice or wheat were also common, and cheaper. For lace, of which there was an abundance in the smart houses, sugar was added to the last rinse and the delicate fabric was then laid between white cloths and placed under books to help it dry flat. 'Very delicate lace may be wound around a glass jar or bottle,' suggested the magazine

Home & Health in 1907, 'then washed [...] leaving it on the glass jar till dry.'

Linen without frills or folds, such as sheets, tablecloths and napkins, was passed through the heavy metal mangles, with two large wooden rollers, to squeeze the water out and flatten it. It was then dried, folded and put into a linen press, a heavy wooden contraption that resembled a huge flower press, to keep it flat.

Pressing the clothes, especially the fine ladies' dresses, was an arduous and fiddly task. Electric irons were invented in 1882 but appeared unsafe, as the few who had used them reported strange noises, flying sparks and blinding flashes of light. A safer one was finally introduced in the US in 1904 but most households carried on with the traditional irons, heated by the fire, until well after the First World War. Most often

An early advertisement for a wrought-iron mangle

the laundry maid would use heavy flat irons, weighing some 10 lb each, which were heated on an ornate stand by the fire. Two or three would be used in rotation so that when one was in use and losing heat the others were warm enough to replace it immediately, preventing unnecessary breaks in the process. Some used a box iron, a hollow metal model that could be filled with hot coals and therefore stay warm for longer and, for the

The Wash House

In the 'big houses', the work was done in a wash house, which was either a few rooms attached to the kitchen or a single-storey building across the yard. It was comprised of a washing room fitted with a series of tubs and coppers, placed at a convenient height for the maid, and a stove to heat the water, unless plumbing allowing hot running water was fitted. The floor was of York stone slabs with a drainage system to draw away the water that slopped on the floor and a flue to draw off the steam. Next door was an ironing room and a drying room, ideally heated with a furnace. The laundry maid spent most of her time in the hot steamy environment, often with her hands plunged into very hot water, and was left with chapped, reddened hands as a result.

For those households that did not boast a laundry maid, there were local laundresses or washerwomen who would take the dirty fabric away on a Monday and return it, washed, starched and pressed, later in the week.

frills and fluting, there was a goffering iron, a strange metal test tube into which a hot metal poker was inserted before the item was wrapped around the outside, although these were dying out by the Edwardian era.

SPRING-CLEANING

When the winter weather turned warmer and the leisured classes began to organize their calendar around forthcoming social events such as the Derby, Cowes week, the London season and the shooting season, life below stairs took on a less monotonous routine. Families with more than one home would move from their country home to their London house for months, taking selected servants with them but leaving others behind on 'boarding wages' to pack up and look after the house. The family exodus would then be the signal for the annual spring clean.

The ornaments, clocks and small items of furniture would first be packed away and the larger furniture draped with sheets, after being cleaned with vinegar and given a new application of beeswax. The loose carpets would be pulled up and taken outside for a thorough beating and the heavy winter curtains taken down from the windows.

The maids would dust and sweep each room before climbing towering stepladders to scrub the ceiling with soda crystals and remove months of grime and grease. Then they would wash down the woodwork using a special paste to whiten the painted areas and get on their hands and knees to scrub the vast wooden floors with soapy water, or soda crystals dissolved in buckets of warm water, before polishing with beeswax. The windows were cleaned with vinegar, the silver and gold plates

---

Skirting Boards

As well as the floors and ceilings, there were hundreds of feet of skirting boards to be scrubbed using pipe clay to remove stains. The following is a cleaning recommendation from *Cassell's Household Guide*:

Scrubbing. – Neglected boards will not come clean without extra pains. If of a very bad colour a mixture of three parts of powdered pipe clay with one of chloride of lime, about the thickness of cream, will be useful. This should be laid on to dry in some time before scrubbing. Or some white sand laid on the brush when scrubbing will remove the dirt. Grease will only yield to fuller's earth spread on the spots for several hours. Well-kept boards, especially in country houses, require nothing but cold water. Soap and soda in hot water make boards black. In scrubbing, only arm's length should be wetted at the time, taking care that the flannel is wrung each time dry of the soiled water. Good bass scrubbing-brushes are more cleansing than those of hair. Vulcanised India-rubber scrubbing-brushes are the best of all, but are rather expensive at the first outlay.

---

were given an extra going over and the hundreds of copper pots in the kitchen scrubbed until they shone. The linen was also examined and any repairs needed were carried out and, finally, the summer curtains were hung.

Spring-cleaning lasted up to four weeks and, according to maid Margaret Thomas, it was 'a great business in those days'.

'As well in the kitchen we had to spring clean whenever the sweep came, which in Yorkshire, where I worked later, where we had the smoke jack, was every six weeks.'

Housemaid's Knee

A 1909 advert shows a smiling maid on her hands and knees, surrounded by furniture covered in white sheets, scrubbing the floor with a brush under the caption 'For spring cleaning, use Calvert's no. 5 carbolic soap' as her benevolent mistress looks on. In reality, few domestic servants would have been so happy about the annual spring clean, which was an arduous process and the young girl in the picture would be quite likely to suffer from housemaid's knee, a painful swelling below the kneecap that afflicted many a maid in service after hours spent on all fours sweeping and scrubbing.

TIPS FOR THE LADY'S MAID

The mistress's personal attendant had her own recipes, or receipts as they were commonly known, for all sorts of things from hair treatments to boot polish, and an array of brushes and other tools to keep her employers smart. Beauty products such as cold cream could be bought or mixed at home and were made from a variety of ingredients including lanolin, almond oil, cocoa butter, coconut oil, white wax, witch hazel and spermaceti – a wax obtained from the head cavity of a sperm whale.

At the end of each day, the lady's maid examined the dresses that had been worn and gently removed any dust or mud with a soft brush or a handkerchief. Footwear was brushed or cleaned with a cloth and kid leather was wiped with milk, to preserve its softness. Bonnets were dusted with a small feather duster, kept for the purpose, and each decorative flower or feather teased back to its intended shape.

As well as a working knowledge of millinery, and a basic understanding of the mixing of lotions and potions, the lady's maid was expected to be an expert hair stylist, often sent on courses to learn the latest trends. Mrs Beeton declared, 'Hairdressing is the most important part of the lady's maid's office.' And she recommended some strange concoction designed to make the lady in question look, if not smell, divine.

A Good Wash for the Hair

INGREDIENTS

1 pennyworth of borax, ½ pint of olive oil, 1 pint of boiling water.

Mode – Pour the boiling water over the borax and oil; let it cool; then put the mixture into a bottle. Shake it before using, and apply it with a flannel. Camphor and borax, dissolved in boiling water and left to cool, make a very good wash for the hair; as also does rosemary water mixed with a little borax. After using any of these washes, when the hair becomes thoroughly dry, a little pomatum or oil should be rubbed in, to make it smooth and glossy.

To make Pomade for the Hair

INGREDIENTS

¼ lb of lard, 2 pennyworth of castor-oil; scent.

Mode – Let the lard be unsalted; beat it up well; then add the castor-oil, and mix thoroughly together with a knife, adding a few drops of any scent that may be preferred. Put the pomatum into pots, which keep well covered to prevent it turning rancid.

Unlike today, hair was seldom washed as Edwardian ladies tended to feel that water was too harsh on their crowning glory. In an interview with *Every Woman's Encyclopaedia*, celebrated soprano Aline Vallandri, described as having 'the Most Wonderful Hair in Europe', said that while cleanliness of hair and scalp were essential, 'I am perfectly certain that much washing of the hair with water is bad. As a matter of fact, I wash my own hair as seldom as possible.'

The secret, she said, was to brush the hair regularly, and to use only clean brushes. 'Every morning when I get up my maid brushes my hair,' she revealed. 'As it is so long I have had to have a specially high stool made to sit on. The maid brushes both my scalp thoroughly and my hair from the roots to the end for half an hour. The other quarter of an hour I devote to dressing it for the day.

'In addition to keeping the hair perfectly clean, this brushing prevents the possibility of any scurf or dandruff – and scurf is death to the hair.' She also, alarmingly, recommended that a compound of mercury be used if 'scurf' did appear.

TIPS FOR THE VALET

Like his female counterpart, the valet took a great deal of time ensuring that his master looked presentable. He would brush his clothes before they were worn and remove grease spots from the collar of his coat on a daily basis, using 'rectified spirit of wine' or ethanol. Boot polish was easy enough to buy, but many a valet prided himself on his own recipe.

An advertisement for Scrubb's, the multipurpose preparation

POLISHING THE 'PLATE'

The footmen or butler were responsible for the appearance of the vast array of silver or silver-plated cutlery known as the 'plate' as well as the table silver. The cutlery would be washed every day and wiped clean with a soft rag or leather cloth. At least once a week it was also cleaned with a paste made from hartshorn powder, otherwise known as ammonium carbonate, which was obtained from the dry distillation of oil found in the horn of a red deer stag. *Cassell's Household Management Guide* maintained, 'Towels boiled in a mixture of a hartshorn powder and water are an excellent rubber for plate in daily use. Rags – old chamber-towels of huckaback (a style of rough weave) are best – boiled in a solution of a quart of water to six ounces of hartshorn powder, are excellent for the purpose.'

110

CHAPTER SIX

Special Occasions

FINE DINING

L ED BY THE love of opulence often displayed by King
Edward VII, the Edwardian upper crust regarded
lavish dinner parties as an essential way of maintaining
their status in society. It was not unusual for a society hostess
to throw two dinner parties a week, and weekend guests would
be treated to two lavish feasts with a lunch party in between.

Margaret Thomas remembered one London house where
entertaining was a weekly event:

> On Friday night we used to have a dinner party. They
> consisted of eight or nine courses and there was usually
> a luncheon party the next day. Everything was prepared
> in the kitchen except salads and desserts. The butler
> had charge of those in his pantry. The cook made all

the etceteras for the table, pastry sticks, candies, salted almonds.

While the downstairs staff dined on cold meats, potatoes and bread, the food which formed the nine or ten courses that graced the dining-room table was of the finest. Oysters, caviar, lobster, truffles, partridge, quail, ptarmigan (white grouse), pressed beef, ham, tongue, chicken, galantines, melons, peaches and nectarines were all ingredients for the Edwardian banquet and a typical dinner party for twenty people would cost up to £60 – five times the annual salary of a scullery maid.

Those below stairs who made these lavish feasts possible would benefit the next day, having an array of leftovers for their own meals in the servants' hall. Even so, it must have been hard for a maid who could barely afford her own stockings to witness the amount of money lavished on these meals, when the wastage in some of the richer households could have fed their family back home for weeks. Margaret Powell began her life in service as a kitchen maid at a house in Adelaide Crescent, Hove. She recalled, 'The amount of food that came into that house seemed absolutely fabulous to me, the amount of food that was eaten and wasted too. They often had a whole saddle of mutton [...] And sirloins. Sometimes with the sirloins they would only eat the undercut and the whole top was left over, so we used to eat that for our dinner. Even so we couldn't eat everything and a lot got thrown away. When I used to think of my family at home where we seldom had enough to eat, it used to break my heart.'

In houses where the staff was not sufficiently large to wait on a dinner party, outside help was brought in on special occasions, often in the form of a local greengrocer. *The Servants' Guide*, published at the end of the nineteenth century, frowned upon this practice: 'The traditional greengrocer from round the corner or a waiter from a confectioner's are not the best class of waiter to employ for the purpose, or from whom good waiting is to be expected,' it sniffed. 'Servants out of place, personally known to the butler, or persons who have formerly been gentlemen's servants, are most to be depended on.' A satirical cartoon in *Punch* magazine suggests the practice was already common in 1876. It shows a haughty-looking shopkeeper and a well-dressed customer and has the caption: 'Comely Greengrocer (who waits on Evening Parties to Lady Customer): "Shall I 'ave the pleasure of meeting you this evening at Lady Fitzwiggle's, Ma'am?"'

In *Cassell's Manners of Modern Society* the writer urges hosts and hostesses never to use anything other than trained waiters at their table: 'Dexterity, rapidity and above all quietness, added to a thorough knowledge of his duties, form the essential requisites of a good waiter. In this department, as in others, only practice makes perfect.' He adds that the common practice of using outdoor staff to serve at big dinners was doomed for disaster:

Hands that have been accustomed to handle spade and besom, to grooming horses, and what not, have not the delicacy of touch necessary for the handling of glass or silver.

[…] Have we ourselves not felt on one occasion a dish of oysters à la crème gliding down the back of our best dress suit and on another had our risible faculties excited and our good manners put to the test at the same time by seeing a young waiter lying prone on the floor, surrounded on all sides by rolls of bread?

Invitations

Invitations to dinner were engraved on card and delivered by the footmen. It was customary to give three weeks' notice, although that rose to five or six by around 1910, and the hostess expected an immediate reply. Guests were expected to arrive fifteen minutes before the appointed time and arriving later was considered a faux pas. A typical invitation might be pre-printed with gaps left for the guest's name and date. For example:

Mr and Mrs William Weatherby-Falks
request the pleasure of
....
company at dinner on
.... at eight o'clock
4 Kensington Mews

Setting the Table

The table was the hostess's chance to make the best first impression and she relied on her footmen or parlourmaid, under the instruction of the butler, to make it spectacular. First, a felt or cloth covering was placed on the table and secured at the legs to stop it slipping. This protected the highly polished surface and deadened the sound of cutlery and china being set down. A starched white damask cloth was laid on top, and the footmen made sure the fold of the cloth was exactly in the centre, with the same drop each side. A dinner plate was then set at each place and the table laid with the cutlery, starting with the soup spoon or oyster fork on the outside and working inwards towards the knife and fork for the main course. Dessert forks and spoons were brought in when required. Wine and water

---

A Guide to Edwardian Servants suggests a bewildering array of glasswear:

> *The glass for water is set nearly in front of the plate, the glass for sauterne at the tip of the soup spoon, and that for sherry between the three, forming a half circle. Back of these, forming a second half circle, with the sauterne glass as the first in the circle, place the glasses for champagne and Burgundy, to accompany the roast and game, respectively.*

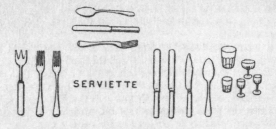

Until quite recently it was usual to place the cheese-knife to the left of the large knives; this arrangement is still often to be seen, and is quite correct. In order to break the line, the knife

SERVIETTE

and fork which come next to those used for fish are sometimes placed rather higher.

How to set the cutlery, according to the
Manual of Household Work and Management *(1913)*

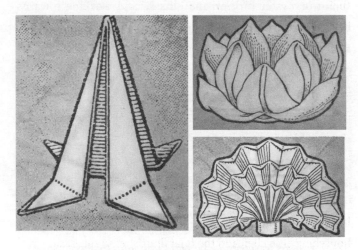

'The Pyramid', 'The Rose and Star' and 'The Fan',
just three methods of serviette-folding from
Mrs Beeton's Book of Household Management

glasses were then set on the table and a bread roll placed to the left of each place in a starched white napkin, half-covered and half visible. Salt and pepper were provided between each two places, flowers placed on the table and silver candelabra placed symmetrically in the centre.

Arrivals

As the guests began to arrive at the front door the footman, or butler where no footman was employed, was on hand to greet them and take their coats. He would then announce their presence to the host and hostess who would be waiting for their guests in the drawing room. Dinner was never served before the last diner arrived and, while the guests chatted with their hosts in the drawing room, the footmen put the finishing touches to the table, filling water glasses, bringing up the butter dishes and possibly laying the first course out, depending on its content. Seafood or canapés would be waiting for the party as they entered but soup would be served after they were seated.

While an air of calm and conviviality reigned in the drawing room, the kitchen was full of frenzied activity with all hands on deck helping the cook, or in the more fashionable households the chef, add the final flourishes to the meal.

At 8 p.m., providing all the guests were in attendance, the butler announced dinner. Each man was paired with a lady to escort to dinner according to their rank. The host would accompany the highest-ranking lady, who would then be seated on his right, while the hostess would take the arm of the highest-ranking man, who sat to her right. The remaining guests were paired off and seated according to their position, with the hostess informing each gentleman of the lady he should escort before the meal was announced.

Inside the dining room the footmen held the chair out for each diner and the host remained standing until all the guests were seated. Constitutional expert Alastair Bruce explains that the posture of the Edwardian upper class meant their spines rarely came in contact with the chair backs: 'The dining room chairs may have a back on them but the back is for the footman to push in and out and not for them to rest their backs on at any time.'

Serving Etiquette

Despite the declining numbers of servants in the early twentieth century, the favoured style of service was *à la Russe* (or Russian style), said to have been introduced by the Russian Ambassador at the Court of Naples. This meant that all courses, except perhaps the first, were served by the footmen, butler and waiting maids, and each plate removed from the table in between.

Contemporary cookery and etiquette expert Janet McKenzie Hill in her *Guide to Edwardian Servants* advised:

It follows, then, that, where this fashion is adopted, a full staff of trained household employees is needed, if the wants of those at table are to be properly supplied. Dinner is the meal for which this formal service is best adapted, and even at dinner it should not be carried out in its entirety unless there be more than one waitress for each eight covers at table, since nothing appears upon the table save the centrepiece (at dinner, a bonbon dish or two is allowable) and the articles that compose the individual covers.

USUAL ORDER OF AN ELABORATE DINNER

Soup.
Fish.
Entrées.
Joints, Removes, or Relevés.
Game or Rôts.
Vegetables.
Entremets.
Cheese.
Dessert.

ADVANTAGES OF DINNER À LA RUSSE

1. The host and hostess are more able to enter into conversation with their guests.
2. It is more rapidly served, and is therefore hotter.
3. The quantity required can be more correctly calculated, as it is not necessary to have a handsome joint.
4. Each diner can take just the amount and the part preferred.
5. The table has more space for decoration.

The advantages of the Russian style, as expressed in the
Manual of Household Work and Management *(1913)*

This labour-heavy convention replaced the French or English style of service, in which the plates were placed in the centre of the table and the roast carved and distributed by the host. For less formal meals the two were combined in what Janet McKenzie Hill termed 'Compromise Style' which was, she wrote, 'a "let down" from the formality of the Russian service and a "let up" to the arduous duties expected of the head of the house at a table served after the English fashion'.

For the servants there were many points of etiquette to remember. The courses were served from the left of the guest either on a pre-prepared plate or by proffering a dish of food from which the guest could serve himself. Wine and other drinks were to be served from the right and each glass filled to no more than two-thirds full. After each course the plates were removed from the right.

Any servant who committed the sin of forgetting a minor point at a dinner party would soon be corrected. According to Margaret Wylie in *Not in Front of the Servants* one parlourmaid in her parents' employ at their London home, known by her surname Allen, passed the port in an anticlockwise direction and was told, 'The *other* way please Allen.' Allen, who had an Irish temper and was incensed by criticism in public, banged the decanter down on the table with a violent crash and marched out, slamming the door behind her. 'Although she had been with us for as long as I could remember, and I was sad to part with "Lizzie" as I called her

out of Mother's earshot, she was dismissed the next morning,'
Wylie recalled.

During courses the butler was the only servant left in the
room, ready to carve the meat on the sideboard and to refill
wine glasses when asked.

Lady Cynthia Asquith commented that although butlers
were undoubtedly 'downstairs despots', the granite-faced,
unflinching stereotype was a rare breed:

> *I very seldom in real life encountered that common stage
> figure, the puma-footed manservant of impalpable presence
> and uncatchable eye. Few butlers, however imposing their
> mien and deportment, were above being visibly, at times
> audibly, amused by dining room jokes or mishaps.*

Diners had to be careful not to upset the servants too, however.
Former butler Charles Cooper revealed in *Life Below Stairs*
how one of his employer's guests, 'a titled lady of a very old
family who was most objectionable', got her just deserts. She
would make it her business to delay the serving of the meal
by refusing to tell the footman whether she would like to
partake in a particular course, much to the annoyance of the
hard-pressed manservant. On one occasion, when she came to
dinner, Cooper 'instructed the footman to place the hot dishes
upon her hand if she still showed the same indifference and this
had the desired effect'.

The Meal

Not only would the dinner party consist of up to ten courses but also, in the finest houses, there would be three choices for several of those courses and a different wine for each. Charles and Elle Thomas-Stanford threw opulent dinner parties at their main house, Preston Manor in Brighton, throughout the first half of the twentieth century. Three of Queen Victoria's daughters, Princesses Beatrice, Alice and Helena, were frequent guests, as was Rudyard Kipling. Below is a breakdown of a typical meal at their palatial home.

First Course
A choice of soups, such as consommé and fish soup,
served with sherry.

Second Course
Fish, such as salmon, mullet or brill, served in a sauce, with
potatoes, and white wine.

Entrée
Vol-au-vents, mutton cutlets or sweetbreads with champagne.

The 'Remove' or 'Relevé'
This was the main course, consisting of a joint of meat or
poultry, served with seasonal vegetables and potatoes that, in
Preston Manor's case, were cut to the size of matchsticks. This
would be served with a good red wine, such as burgundy.

The Game Course

Duck, pheasant, partridge or snips, served with thinly sliced fried potatoes known as 'game chips', washed down with claret.

The Entremêts

From the French for 'between servings', this was a choice of three different types of dish – a vegetable dish, a sweet dish such as a fruit tart, or a savoury dish such as sardines or cheese.

Ices

Before this course, the table was cleared and fresh wine glasses placed on the table. The footmen then brought in some fingerbowls for the guests and laid dessert cutlery.

Port, Fruit and Nuts

When the ices were finished the dishes were removed and the dessert plates left in case anyone had any room for the fruit and nuts that followed. Port and Madeira were then served and the ladies retired to the drawing room leaving, as they had entered, in order of rank, while the men stayed over port, Madeira or brandy, and smoked cigars.

Coffee

Served to both parties in their respective rooms.

ENTRÉES.

1.—Toulouse Pasty.   2.—Fillets of Beef.   3.—Beef Galantine.   4.—Zéphires of Duck.
5.—Mutton Cutlets in Aspic.   6.—Sauté of Veal.   7.—Chartreuse of Pheasant.
8.—Curried Veal.   9.—Chicken Médaillons.   10.—Veal Stew.

Just some of the entrées an Edwardian diner might expect, as illustrated in Mrs Beeton's Book of Household Management

After the ladies had retreated the men were allowed to smoke. In some houses the men retired to a smoking room or library for their nightcap and cigar, but most stayed at the dining table, where they could discuss politics, business and other subjects considered unsuitable for the delicate female ear.

During the postprandial separation the butler was expected to be on hand in case further refreshments were required and the downstairs staff stayed on duty until the last guest had retired. According to Cynthia Asquith, hostesses were frequently upset by this 'segregation of the sexes, often of long duration, for most hosts seemed to sit an unconscionable time over their port liqueurs and cigars'. She added that 'the mistress of the house would worry if her staff were kept up too late'.

The following is a typical menu suggested by Edwardian cookery writer Janet McKenzie Hill.

Oysters. Brown-bread Sandwiches.
Consommé. Pulled Bread. Olives. Celery.
Baked Turbans of Fish. Potato Diamonds with Peas.
Cucumber Salad.
Sweetbread-and-Mushroom Croquettes. Asparagus Tips.
Roast Turkey. Cranberry Jelly. Mashed Potato. Fried Egg Plant.
Roman Punch.
Broiled Fillets of Venison. Red Currant Jelly in Rice Cups.
    Chicory Salad.

Macedoine of Fruit in Jelly (Individual Moulds). Whipped
Cream.
Bonbons. Salted Almonds.
Coffee.

ROMAN PUNCH

Although more of a drink than a dish, Punch Romaine, or
Roman Punch, was a popular addition to the Edwardian dinner
party. It was served as the sixth course at the final dinner on
the *Titanic* in 1912, after the main course of roast duckling and
apple sauce and before roast squab (pigeon), asparagus salad
and foie gras.

INGREDIENTS

    6 cups crushed ice

    2 cups champagne or sparkling wine

    1 cup white wine

    ⅓ cup freshly squeezed orange juice

    2 tablespoons lemon juice

    Orange peel, slivered, optional

    1 cup sugar

    ½ cup water

METHOD

1. In a large saucepan, combine the sugar and water and cook over medium heat, stirring gently until the sugar is completely dissolved.

2. Bring to a boil and simmer for one minute until the syrup is clear. Leave to cool.

3. Combine the crushed ice, simple syrup, champagne, white wine, orange juice and lemon juice. Mix until mixture is well combined.

4. Spoon the mixture into individual dessert cups. Drizzle with rum, if desired, and garnish with a sliver of orange peel. Serve immediately.

QUAIL AND BEEF PUDDING

This meaty creation was the speciality of former servant girl Rosa Lewis who became a celebrity in the early 1900s through her rags-to-riches story. She started in domestic service as a teenager and worked her way up through the ranks to become chief cook for the wealthy Duc d'Orléans. Having studied French cuisine she left service to start a business catering for dinner parties at rich households and was so popular that she had to employ teams of cooks. Her fame spread and she even cooked for King Edward VII, who was said to be impressed.

In 1902, she bought her own hotel, The Cavendish, in London's Jermyn Street. Thanks to her management and her legendary cooking skills, it soon became one of the most exclusive hotels in London and earned her the nickname, the Duchess of Jermyn Street. The classic TV series, *Duchess of Duke Street*, was based on her life. And if there is any doubt that a lowly servant girl could improve her lot with hard work and determination, the proof is in the pudding.

INGREDIENTS

50g / 2 oz butter

Pinch of fine herbs

12 quail breasts, skin removed

450g / 1lb Aberdeen Angus beef, fat removed, cut into thin slices

75g / 3 oz button mushrooms

50g / 2 oz shallots, sliced

150ml / 5 fl oz fresh orange juice

1 sprig of fresh thyme

2 tablespoons brandy

Salt and freshly milled black pepper

150ml/ 5 fl oz game sauce

225g / 8 oz suet pastry (*see* pastry)

METHOD

1. Melt the butter in a large frying pan, add the herbs, quail breasts, mushrooms and shallots and fry for six minutes. Remove the quail and set aside.

2. Add the orange juice, thyme, brandy and seasoning to

the pan, bring to the boil and simmer for at least twenty minutes until the liquid is reduced by half. Add the game sauce and reduce by half again.

FOR THE PASTRY
   220g / 8 oz self-raising flour
   1 level tsp baking powder
   110g / 4 oz beef suet
   Salt & freshly ground white pepper
   Pinch of mace
   Pinch of ground rosemary
   60 ml approx of cold water to mix

1. Sieve the flour, salt, pepper and spices. Toss in the beef suet and stir in with a fork. Make a well in the centre and add just enough water to make workable dough. Knead for a few minutes and use immediately.

2. Line a 20-cm/ 8-in. pudding basin with the suet pastry and lay the quail meat and beef, before pouring on the prepared sauce. Cover the top of the basin with suet pastry and seal. Gently brush the top with melted butter and cover with a few layers of cooking foil. Steam the pudding in a covered saucepan for two hours, topping up the pan with water as necessary.

Making 'Game Chips'

First of all you peeled the potatoes, then you got a clean tea cloth and laid it out full length on the table and sliced the potatoes by hand so thinly that when you held them up you could see right through them. They were like little rashers of wind. Then you covered them up with another cloth until they dried. Then you melted fat – lard not dripping because that was too coloured – in a frying pan, a very deep one, and when it was boiling and blue smoke came off, you dropped these crisps in, one by one, because if you dropped two in at a time they stuck together, they wouldn't separate out. By the time you got the last one in, the first ones were already cooked, so it was a mad rush to drop them in and get the first lot out again.

Margaret Powell, *Below Stairs*

THE SEASON

From the middle of May to the middle of August, society families moved to their London homes for the 'Season'. The summer was an endless round of balls, dinner parties, trips to the ballet and the opera, racing at Ascot and Epsom and the Henley Regatta. For the London staff it meant a hugely increased workload, more dinner parties to cater for and the occasional ball too. With so much socializing, the maid's bedtime was often midnight or later and she would have to be up with the lark to scrub floors and black-lead the kitchen range. The master and mistress often brought servants with them to help out during the Season, leaving a skeleton staff at the country estate to keep the house ticking over, but it was non-stop work from dusk to dawn nonetheless.

Arthur Inch, in service for more than fifty years, was a footman at Londonderry House during one London Season, and spent a busy day wearing a pedometer as he rushed up and down the stairs and along the vast corridors. He calculated that he had walked eighteen miles without ever leaving the house.

As well as the extra dinners, there were hundreds of balls during the London Season. The parents of a debutante who was 'coming out' that year often rented in the capital and threw a ball to introduce their daughter to Society and, more importantly, to eligible bachelors. There could be as many as four balls in one night. For the servants, this meant laying on a lavish supper, and staying up very late indeed. In 1912, Lady Charlotte Bonham Carter's mother threw a ball in a house in Eaton Square she had taken for her daughter's first season. 'Supper had to be taken downstairs unless it was a very grand house, like Surrey House,' remembered Lady Charlotte in *Lost Voices of the Edwardians*. 'Supper generally began at twelve and might consist of a clear soup, quails with white grapes and potatoes. It was a light but really delicious meal and you could take it whenever you liked.' The servants who were up until the early hours clearing up must have been pleased this was a rare event.

Footman Eric Horne revealed in his memoirs *What the Butler Winked At*, 'A London season is very tiring to servants. There is not only the day work but the night work as well. They would keep out regularly until one, two or three o'clock but we had to start work at the same time as the other servants. Often during the London season we were kept so short of our hours of sleep that I used to go to sleep on the carriage.'

The season ended in August when the grouse-shooting season began and most men went north for shooting parties.

SHOOTING PARTIES

The Edwardian shooting parties were lavish events that required yet more catering from the servants. The valets or footmen would accompany the men in order to load their guns and the maids would be up at the crack of dawn to cut sandwiches for the party. When the men returned with the spoils, the hallboy or scullery maid would be charged with plucking the birds and hanging them in the pantry or game larder until cook was ready to prepare them for dinner. As the shooters left early, the butler and remaining footman would take their lunch out to them on the moors or they would return to the house for a more substantial meal.

The Duke of Portland's footman Frederick Gorst remembered shooting parties at Welbeck Abbey. 'We footmen

Average cost of goods 1909–1910		
	Price per lb (unless otherwise stated)	Today's Price
Beef Sirloin	9*d*.	£2.14
Beef Buttock	10*d*.	£2.38
Beef Tongue	2*s*. 6*d*. each	£7.13
Venison	1*s*.–2*s*.	£2.85
Lamb leg (English)	1*s*.	£2.85
Lamb leg (New Zealand)	9½*d*.	£2.26
Hare	3*s*. 6*d*. each	£9.99
Chicken	2*s*. 6*d*. each	£7.13
Duckling	2*s*.–3*s*. each	£5.71–£8.56
Grouse	3*s*. 6*d*. per brace	£9.99
Quail	1*s*. each	£2.85
Snipes	2*s*. each	£5.71
Widgeon	1*s*. each	£2.85
Loaf of bread	2½*d*. each	60p
Butter	1*s*. 2*d*.	£3.33
Sugar	3*d*.	71p
Tea	1*s*. 6*d*.	£4.28
Potatoes	10*d*. (20 lb)	£2.38
Cheese	6*d*.	£1.43

Figures taken from Mrs Beeton's *Book of Household Management* and the Black Country Living Museum served them from our stations at the sideboard which held roast game in season, leg of lamb, game pie, roast chicken and roast ham. There were always platters of egg Rochambeau, fish, a garnished entrée of chicken en gelée and salad. The sweet was often rice pudding.'

CHAPTER SEVEN

Code of Conduct

As SOON AS ANY servant took a position in a household they were subject to a long list of dos and don'ts – some issued by their mistress and some by their downstairs superiors. Most establishments had the rules written on cardboard or framed paper that was then hung in the kitchen or in the servants' hall. Those 'rules' that were not on the list, and which differed from house to house, they would pick up along the way, it was hoped before their ignorance of them got them into trouble.

Most of the codes of conduct revolved around being as unobtrusive as possible. Although Edwardian families liked to be able to afford the armies of maids that ran around below stairs, they didn't wish to see or hear them at any time. Most of the lowlier servants never spoke to their mistress or master, even if their paths crossed, and this was encouraged in the many regulations recommended at the time. The kitchen staff rarely left the basement and should a parlourmaid or chambermaid pass a member of the family they were expected to stand against the wall and look down at the floor.

One contemporary servants' guide made it quite clear that you should, 'Always "give room": that is, if you encounter one of your betters in the house or on the stairs, you are to make yourself as invisible as possible, turning yourself toward the wall and averting your eyes.'

A booklet produced by the Ladies' Sanitary Association in 1901, entitled *Rules For the Manners of Servants in Good Families*, laid out a list of rules which would have made a young girl's head spin. What follows are a few of the major ones.

- Do not walk in the garden unless permitted, or unless you know that all the family are out; and be careful to walk quietly when there; on no account be noisy.
- Noisiness is considered bad manners.
- Always move quietly about the house, and do not let your voice be heard by the family unless necessary.
- Never sing or whistle at your work where the family would be likely to hear you.
- Do not call out from room to room and if you are a housemaid, be careful not only to do your work quietly but to keep out of sight as much as possible.
- Never begin to talk to the ladies and gentlemen, unless it be to deliver a message or ask a necessary question.

- Do not talk to your fellow servants or the children of the family in the passages or sitting rooms, or in the presence of ladies and gentlemen.

- Always answer when you receive an order or a reproof either, 'yes ma'am' or 'I am very sorry ma'am' to show you have heard.

- Should you be required to walk with a lady or gentleman, in order to carry a parcel or otherwise, always keep a few paces behind.

- *Do not* smile at droll stories told in your presence or seem in any way to notice, or enter into, the family conversation, or the talk at table, or with visitors.

This is a small sample of the strict regulations governing the daily lives of servants. Other requirements included being punctual at mealtimes, having all doors locked by a certain time such as 10.30 p.m., when the servants' hall also had to be cleared and closed, and paying for breakages out of meagre wages. Gambling, swearing and drinking to excess were banned and the female staff were forbidden to smoke.

The maids were considered so lowly that should they need to hand a family member or visitor a letter or parcel, they were to do so on a silver platter to minimize the risk of physical contact. If they were obliged to lift something by hand, they were to lay it on a table nearest the recipient. This was one rule that kitchen maid Margaret Langley, later Powell, fell foul of when she started out in Hove. One morning, while she was cleaning the front door, the newsboy came by with the papers. As she took them her mistress, Mrs Clydesdale, descended the stairs and Margaret offered her the papers:

> *She looked at me as if I were something subhuman . . . She didn't speak a word, she just stood there looking at me as if she couldn't believe someone like me was walking an' breathing . . . I couldn't think what was wrong. Then at last she spoke. She said, 'Langley, never, never on any occasion ever hand anything to me in your bare hands, always use a silver salver. Surely you know better than that.' I thought it was terrible. Tears started to trickle down my cheeks; that someone could think that you were so low that you couldn't even hand them anything out of your hands without it first being placed on a silver salver.*

FOLLOWERS

A ban on 'followers' was common to the majority of houses. The main reason this rule was put in place was to discourage boyfriends and potential suitors to the girls from coming to the house but the term also took in relations and friends, who were seen as an unwelcome distraction from daily chores. *Cassell's Household Guide* declared, 'Whether "followers" are allowed is a question often put by a servant on applying for a situation. Except under very rare circumstances, it is better to disallow the privilege.' It continued: 'While speaking on this subject, we may add that the word "followers" has a very elastic meaning, and as it is difficult to draw a line between those that are unobjectionable and otherwise, no hardship can be felt in refusing to admit visitors to the kitchen save upon express permission.'

With one evening off a week and a chance to go to church on Sunday it was tricky for the domestic staff to see their family, let alone their friends. And finding a potential spouse was incredibly difficult for some. Even within the household, any servant found 'fraternizing' with the opposite sex faced instant dismissal. It's a wonder any of the young maids ever found a suitor at all.

Violet Turner recalled to author Frank Dawes, 'We weren't allowed a young man near the house, but I always let the cook's young man in the back door on Friday evenings.'

Kate Brown revealed she was sacked from her parlour-maid's job in 1911 for allowing her boyfriend into the house: 'Of course it was forbidden in those days in case your boyfriend might be a burglar. They could never imagine a servant choosing someone respectable.' Her future husband was, actually, a baker from Fulham Road.

CRIME AND PUNISHMENT

Breaking the rules, or being seen to, meant swift and often severe punishment. This could range from a 'tongue-lashing', usually enough to put the wind up the inexperienced maid, to dismissal with no references, or 'characters', a terrifying prospect for most domestic servants. The favourite sanction was the denial of the little time off they had, as there were so few pleasures in life. One servant recalled losing her day off for the heinous crime of feeding lumps of sugar from her own ration to a black horse on the farm where she worked.

Some were a little more eccentric in their punishments. The 5th Duke of Portland, William John Cavendish-Bentinck-Scott, became a recluse in the late nineteenth century and hated his female servants to see him. If he passed any of them in the corridors, he sent them outside to skate on a specially constructed ice rink.

While the domestic staff devoted sixteen hours a day to backbreaking chores, mistresses often rewarded their efforts with suspicion of dishonesty and idleness. Some would employ subterfuge to test the honesty of the staff. The most common method was to slip coins under rugs and down the side of upholstered chairs. If the coin was removed and not declared, the housemaid was deemed to be a thief and, if the coin was undiscovered, she was a shirker.

RELIGIOUS FERVOUR

Society households often used religion as a tool for keeping their domestic staff in check. By drumming passages from the scriptures about hard work and cleanliness into them they reinforced the message that the hierarchy that kept the upper-class employers at the top and the work-ravaged servants at the bottom was all part of God's plan. Employers liked to believe they were the guardians of their servants' morals, and that they needed to be taught how to behave by their educated betters. 'They didn't worry about the long hours you put in, the lack of freedom and the poor wages, so long as you worked hard and you knew that God was in Heaven and that He'd arranged for it that you worked down below and laboured, and that they lived upstairs in comfort and luxury, that was alright with them,' wrote Margaret Powell. 'I used to think how incongruous it was when the Reverend used to say morning prayers and just before they were over, he'd say, "Now let us all count our blessings." I thought, well, it would take a lot longer to count yours than it would mine.'

Religious mantras hung around the servants' area included such messages as 'Cleanliness comes next to Godliness' and, from Ecclesiastes, 'Whatever your hand finds to do, do it with all your might, for in the grave, where you are going, there is neither working nor planning nor knowledge nor wisdom.' No doubt they omitted those less convenient to their way of thinking, such as the famous line from Exodus which commands that Christians should 'Remember the Sabbath day by keeping it holy,' and continues, 'On it you shall not do any work, neither you, nor your son or daughter, nor your manservant or maidservant.'

Christian societies were keen to get in on the act and issued numerous pamphlets for mistresses and maids on the subject of servants' morals. In 1890 the Society for Promoting Christian Knowledge published a booklet which advised staff not to worry about wages as a 'safe, happy home is of greater consequence', not to lose their temper if the steps they had just scrubbed were instantly splattered with mud, not to gossip with tradesmen or servants and not to read 'silly sensational stories' in the 'poisonous publications which are brought to the back doors of gentlemen's homes'. Above all, it counselled, a servant must remember to pray carefully and regularly.

In his memoirs, Eric Horne recalled the country house of an unnamed peer where he worked as a footman, and the staff having to sit opposite the family during the Sunday service. 'One Sunday the Bold Bad Baron sent for the butler and asked him if we had been drinking too much beer as he noticed several of the men were asleep during the sermon. The parson was brother to the Baron, the living was in his gift, so of course he preached a sermon to please him; generally about the lower orders being submissive to their betters. No wonder we fell asleep.'

CODE OF CONDUCT

ADDRESSING THE SERVANTS

Those who lived upstairs were also expected to adhere to strict rules of etiquette in their treatment of the staff, particularly in how each member was addressed. The name used by the master and mistress was part of the rigid hierarchy and it would be an insult to the higher ranks to stray from the usual titles.

The following is a guide on how to address servants adapted from the Channel Four series *An Edwardian Country House*.

- The Butler should be addressed courteously by his surname.
- The Housekeeper should be given the title of 'Missus …', regardless of marital status.
- The Chef de Cuisine should be addressed as such, or by the title 'Monsieur …'.
- It is customary for your Lady's Maid to be given the title of 'Miss …', regardless of whether she is single or married. It is however acceptable for the mistress to address her by her Christian name.
- It is very much the custom in the old houses that lower servants, when entering into service, adopt new names given to them by their masters. You may follow this tradition and rename certain members of your staff. Common names for matching footmen are James and John. Emma is popular for housemaids.

● It is not expected that you take the trouble to remember the names of all your staff. Indeed, in order to avoid obliging you to converse with them, lower servants will endeavour to make themselves invisible to you. As such they should not be acknowledged.

The housekeeper should be given the title of 'Missus ...'

CHAPTER EIGHT

Hiring and Firing

OR MANY OF the lower female staff, the initial interview for the job was the only time they would speak to the mistress or, in some of the larger houses, see her at all. Margaret Powell remembered her first interview for a kitchen maid's position in Hove, when she was fifteen. Her mother came with her and they were let in by the front door. 'In all the time I worked there, that was the only time I ever went in by the front door.'

Margaret and her mother were shown into a nursery where the mistress of the house interrogated them. 'My mother did all the talking because I was overcome with wonder at this room, for although it was only a nursery, you could have put all the three rooms we lived in into it. Also I was overcome with shyness; I suffered agonies of self-consciousness in those days. And the lady, Mrs Clydesdale, looked me up and down as though I was something at one of those markets, you know one of those slave markets.' As the rules and conditions were outlined, Margaret's spirits sank and she said, 'I felt I was in jail at the finish.' But like many girls, she was not given a choice. Her mother had made up her mind that she would take the job, and that was what she did.

Positions often came to the attention of potential candidates by word of mouth, via a relative, friend or neighbour who already worked there. For a teenager looking for their first job particularly, it would be easier if someone within the existing staff 'spoke for' him or her. One Norwich maid recalled entering into service in Kent after she was recommended by a neighbour's daughter who already worked there. After packing her things into a wicker basket, she travelled up to London and on to Beckenham. 'I quite expected a Rolls Royce to meet me at the station,' she said in *Cap and Apron*. 'Instead of that it was the gardener with the wheelbarrow.'

Mrs Beeton advised that hiring the staff was 'one of those duties in which the judgement of the mistress must be keenly exercised'. And she recommended that the best way to find new servants was to ask among friends, acquaintances and tradesmen.

She also counselled mistresses to be absolutely clear what the job entailed:

> *We would here point out an error – and a grave one it is – into which some mistresses fall. They do not, when*

engaging a servant, expressly tell her all the duties which she will be expected to perform. This is an act of omission severely to be reprehended. Every portion of work which the maid will have to do, should be plainly stated by the mistress, and understood by the servant. If this plan is not carefully adhered to, domestic contention is almost certain to ensue, and this may not be easily settled; so that a change of servants, which is so much to be deprecated, is continually occurring.

Cassell's Household Guide goes one step further, castigating employers for not being candid with applicants for a housemaid's job from the outset:

Many ladies, when engaging a housemaid, hold out the 'lightness of the work' as an inducement to get the place filled. Consequently, no sphere of domestic service is so crowded with young women in delicate health as that of the housemaid. Good health is, nevertheless, indispensable to the fit discharge of all kinds of labour.

But word of mouth was not the only way that servants found places. Many advertised their qualities in *The Times*, since it was the preferred paper of the upper classes and offered potential staff the opportunity to place a free advert, paying only when a position was secured. A persuasive argument put forward in an

WANT PLACES.
(THREE LINES, 1s. 6L)

TRAVELLING MAID, experienced. Recommended by a lady. Speaks Italian, French, English. Good packer, hairdresser, needlewoman.—M.A., Sinclair, 46, High-street, Notting-hill-gate.

MAID. Very good needlewoman, traveller, and packer. Most attentive in illness.—E. H., Old Rectory, Goring-on-Thames.

MAID (UNDER), or Maid to grown children. Age 19. First place. Four years' dressmaking. Sister can be interviewed in London.—A. Gee., 4, Merrion-square, Dublin, Ireland.

DRESSMAKER (thoroughly experienced) at ladies' houses or at home. Town or country.—Mrs. Peach, 8, Badsworth-road, Camberwell.

DRESSMAKER (FRENCH). Making and remodelling dresses. Ladies' houses. Not object to country.—A. E., 23, Montpelier-place, Brompton-road, S.W.

IN-DOOR SERVANT (thorough) where assistance is given. Age 48, height 5ft. 9in, active and obliging. 12 months' good personal character.—C. G., 2, Nursery-villa, Bounds-green, New Southgate, N

VALET to an invalid gentleman. Thorough all-round English manservant and qualified male nurse. Highly recommended.—Valet, 2, North-row, Earl's-court. S.W.

COACHMAN. Age 35. Married. Town or country. Pair or single. 3 years' character, 4½ previous.—W. M., 9, Montpelier-street, S.W. No circulars.

COACHMAN. Ride and drive single and pair. Good personal character. Knows town well. Age 30. Light weight. Married, one child.—W. R., 41, Claton-mews, Cadogan-square.

GARDENER (HEAD WORKING) Age 40. One year's good character, 5 years' previous. Wife experienced Laundress. One girl, age 17.—G. Barker, Down-house, Down, Kent.

HALL BOY, in nobleman's family. Age 15. Good character. Some knowledge of work.—Richards, Owston, Doncaster.

Positions wanted, from a 1902 edition of The Times

editorial suggested that servants engaged through a newspaper which cost 3*d.* instead of the rags that cost a mere 1*d.* were likely to find themselves a comfortable position in a family of 'the best class' who kept many servants. 'They are not cheap, common-place people, but good families having fine establishments and too anxious to have everything of the best not to keep plenty of servants for the work to be done.'

Agencies, known as 'registry offices', were also possible sources for work, although in the Victorian era they had often been fronts for recruiting prostitutes for low-class brothels in big cities. The more respectable establishments offered country girls who were seeking work accommodation, albeit sparse,

> **Mop Fairs**
>
> Throughout the eighteenth and nineteenth centuries, in rural areas, girls could also be hired at 'Mop fairs' in the market places. These were colourful, noisy affairs full of young girls dressed in the finest clothes they had and enjoying a day out and a good natter. Agricultural workers also wandered about, hoping for employment, and masters and mistresses had the opportunity to scrutinize and interview the good, hard-working country girls they believed made the most industrious maids. By the beginning of the twentieth century, however, these hiring fairs were dying out.

while they awaited appointment. Mistresses could then come to the premises and interview candidates in dedicated booths. The leading agency in the early1900s was Mrs Hunt's, in Duke Street, London. Established in 1896 by Mrs Ellen Hunt, it offered butlers, housekeepers, parlourmaids, footmen and cooks to fine households on a 'no placement, no fee' basis and its stairwell boasted a 'roll of honour', detailing the most illustrious clients and the impressive length of service of their upper servants. Virginia Woolf referred to the employment agency in her diaries, in 1938, when she wrote, 'Here's the unusual stir and bother: Nessa back tomorrow, Flossie ill: am I to go Hunting?' The company survived until 2005 when it was taken over and became Top Notch Staffing Ltd. Mrs Massey's ran on similar lines, operating first in Derby in the mid-nineteenth century and later expanding to a shop in London. In the 1890s owner Ernest Massey, who inherited the business from his mother, introduced the all-important 'Certificates of Character', or references.

REFERENCES

Being sacked from a good position was a threat hanging over domestic staff at all times and they could be dismissed for the smallest slight or misdemeanour. But their biggest fear would be leaving without good references, effectively rendering them incapable of finding work elsewhere. An unjust reference was punishable with a £20 fine but in order to enforce this rule, the injured servant would have to prove malice, which was not an easy thing to do. At the same time, the master or mistress giving the reference was legally obliged to tell the truth about any character flaw that may affect future work, such as dishonesty or drunkenness, so generosity was not an option.

In 1923, a Government committee recognized the harm that could be done to a servant's prospects under this system. 'Our attention has constantly been drawn to the extent to which a maid's future is at the mercy of an unjust or spiteful employer who by withholding a reference, or giving an unfair or prejudiced account of her, may easily render her chances of obtaining desirable employment very small.' The committee recommended that 'unless an employer has sufficiently definite grounds for dissatisfaction to be prepared to state them in writing, and to tell the maid at least what their general nature is, she should give a formal reference only and refrain from criticism or comment unless pressed for further details'. However, without any legal sanction to help the maids, there was still no official protection against character slurs.

Mrs Beeton on Giving References:
IN GIVING A CHARACTER, it is scarcely necessary to say that the mistress should be guided by a sense of strict justice. It is not fair for one lady to recommend to another, a servant she would not keep herself. The benefit, too, to the servant herself is of small advantage; for the failings which she possesses will increase if suffered to be indulged with impunity. It is hardly necessary to remark, on the other hand, that no angry feelings on the part of a mistress towards her late servant, should ever be allowed, in the slightest degree, to influence her, so far as to induce her to disparage her maid's character.

FALLEN WOMEN

The need for good characters before landing any position kept many a servant in an unhappy home for longer than they would

MISS WRIGHT'S AGENCY,

CONDUCTED BY
[MISS J. A. WRIGHT.

TELEGRAPHIC ADDRESS:
"WRIGHT'S AGENCY, STOCKTON-ON-TEES."
(THREE WORDS.)

All communications and addresses
sent are strictly confidential.

DERBY HOUSE,

HARTINGTON ROAD,

STOCKTON-ON-TEES,

Nov. 14th 1895

Re Margaret Seaton

Applying for situation as Under housemaid

MADAM,

The Servant above-mentioned has applied to me for a situation, and has referred to you for character.

I shall be much obliged if you will be so good as to inform me how long and in what capacity she was in your service; whether you found her honest, truthful, steady, industrious, respectful, and competent (mentioning any points in regard to domestic ability, commendable or otherwise, as may seem to you desirable); and whether you think she is capable of undertaking the duties of the position mentioned above, which she desires to fill.

Awaiting your esteemed reply,

I am, Madam,

Your obedient Servant,

J. A. WRIGHT.

Mrs. York

'Honest, truthful, steady, industrious, respectful, and competent' –
the qualities needed for a good reference

Situations Wanted

IN CRICKLEWOOD OR HENDON.

PARLOURMAID; Age 26. 2 years Character. £18.

HOUSE-PARLOURMAID ; Very superior; Tall; no fringe. Age 23. 3 years Character. £14. 16s.

GENERAL OR PLAIN COOK. Age 23. 13 months' Character. £17.

GENERAL where House-maid is kept. Age 23. 2 years Character. Disengaged 3rd. April.

YOUNG GENERAL COUNTRY GIRL. Age 18. 12 months' character. £10. Apply Mrs. Johnson's High Class Registry, 39, High Road, Kilburn.

The importance of Character: servants advertising their qualities in a London newspaper

have liked. Even so, dismissal could be instant and unfair, with no repercussions for the quick-tempered employer, and would leave a young girl on the street. Many of these youngsters ended up in brothels, cajoled, tricked or bullied into prostitution. In the publication *How to Improve the Conditions of Domestic Servants*, one male servant voiced his concern that the sacking without references of 'many poor servant girls' meant they were being 'led into immorality and thrown on to the street of London'. Many of the servant registry offices were actually recruitment fronts for city brothels and older women were often employed to scout the railway stations and streets for naive-looking, out-of-towners on their own, who would then be offered a place to stay and find themselves forced into prostitution.

Kitty Marion recalled a close shave with one such woman after a trip to visit a friend in London, on her Sunday afternoon off. Kitty befriended the woman who had asked her for directions and was offered a bed for the night in a flat in Gray's Inn Road. On the way there, they bumped into two men and Kitty struck up a conversation with one of them. He edged her out of earshot before asking 'Is that woman a friend of yours?' Kitty continued, 'I was surprised and told him how I had met her, and that she had invited me home, whereupon he became most concerned and said, "Little girl, she's no fit companion for you, come along, here's your bus,"' and he hailed one. He helped me up the stairs and said "Good night, dear" as if he'd known me all my life.' Telling friends later she admitted, 'I was a greenhorn. I had no ideas that women had "evil designs" on others. This one was so ladylike too.'

MOVING UP AND MOVING ON

In the largest households, a lower servant might be able to progress through the ranks, learning their trade at the elbow of those above them. However, if the house was a good, comfortable one, held in affection by those who worked there, the upper servants were less likely to leave and the lower servants would be obliged to seek work elsewhere in order to 'better themselves'.

Having worked for three years as a kitchen maid, Margaret Powell applied for a job as a cook in Kensington. Although she was only eighteen she lied about her age, telling the mistress of the house, Lady Gibbons, that she was twenty, in order to seem more experienced. She had come a long way from the terrified teenager who had refused to speak at her first interview. During the 'usual interrogation', she was asked how much money she expected:

> I heard a voice that didn't sound like mine saying, 'Forty pounds.' 'Forty pounds!' she echoed, as if I'd asked for the Crown Jewels. There was a pause as if she thought I would reconsider it. I didn't. 'Yes', I said, 'and I want a whole day off a month.' Her face fell still further. 'If I give you a whole day off every month,' she said, 'the housemaid and the parlourmaid will want one too.' I said nothing. Just sat silent.

Margaret got the job, and on her own terms.

Getting a better job was not the only reason for moving on, however. For the maids, the most common reason for leaving service was marriage. In 1844, Lavinia Jane Watson, mistress of Rockingham Castle, was dismayed that her lady's maid Lloyd was ill. It turned out she was merely too nervous to tell her employer of her decision to leave and eventually the housekeeper, Mrs Champion, had to do it for her. 'Champion broke the ice about

Lloyd, who wishes to marry Mr Lloyd,' wrote Mrs Watson in her diary. 'And as it incurred her leaving me, she was in low spirits. Had an interview with the bride and comforted her.'

The expectation for maids to leave in order to marry continued well into the twentieth century. Margaret Powell commented in her memoirs on the hypocritical attitude of the upper classes, who encouraged their own daughters to meet young men at parties and balls while the servants were allowed 'no followers'. And yet they saw marriage as the only acceptable reason for a young girl to leave service.

'It was a funny thing that although none on them like you to leave if you were going to another job, if you left to get married, it was a totally different thing,' she wrote. 'It was acceptable and it was respectable. And yet the business of getting a young man was not respectable, and one's employers tended to degrade any relationship.'

DISMISSAL

Although the work was exhausting and the conditions often meagre, the alternative to a life in service, for many, didn't bear thinking about. Servants would put up with a harsh or mean mistress for months or years rather than leave without a reference but being dismissed for a minor misdemeanour was all too common. Hannah Cullwick, whose diaries were edited by Liz Stanley in 1984, was employed as a maid at Aqualate Hall in Staffordshire in the mid twentieth century and lost her position after her mistress spied her and another maid laughing while going about their chores. 'I got on very well as under-housemaid for eight months, but Lady Boughey saw me and another playing as we was cleaning our kettles (we had about 16 to clean, they belong'd to the bedroom),' she wrote. 'I was vex'd to leave. I ax'd Lady Boughey if she would please forgive me and let me stop. But she said "NO" very loudly.'

Bad behaviour, real or perceived, wasn't the only reason for dismissal. Hannah also recalled being let go because she was considered too young and the aforementioned Lavinia Watson recalled in her diary how the replacement for her treasured lady's maid Lloyd lasted just two days. 'Short old fashioned mincing body – won't do,' she wrote, although she had the grace to admit that, having dismissed the unfortunate Stephenson, 'her humble resigned manner on the occasion almost made me feel a lump, and yet I am sure I have never felt less fascinated by anyone.'

The household uprooting for the Season could be enough to see a maid left jobless. Margaret Thomas remembered how she was summoned by the Lady of the House, a rare honour, only to be given her notice. 'When the family were going to Scotland for the shooting season the Lady sent for me and told me they weren't taking me as I wasn't strong enough for the hard life there,' she recalled. 'I was upset because I was looking forward to the visit . . . But I appreciated the fact that the Lady told me herself, for it was the only time I saw her.'

THE OLD RETAINERS

For those who became too old or ill to do their jobs effectively, their fortunes depended on the largesse of their employers and their own financial prudence throughout their service. Giving evidence before the Royal Commission on the Aged Poor in 1893, Joseph Chamberlain outlined a sorry fate for some, commenting that households were reluctant to hire anyone over fifty and that 'accordingly almost by necessity of the case, they will have to go to the workhouse'.

But long and loyal service often paid dividends in old age, with employers making provision for their 'old retainers'. Many an ageing housekeeper, butler or gardener was retired to a gatehouse or to a cottage in the grounds and, in some cases, was employed in much lighter duties, such as gatekeeping, sewing or providing sage advice for the younger servants. At Welbeck Abbey, the 6th Duke of Portland built almshouses for retiring staff on the estate. He was a huge fan of racing, won the Derby twice and kept one thoroughbred, St Simon, who sired numerous champions. Having paid for the building work out of the proceeds of his hobby, he named his charitable housing 'The Winnings'.

But it was not just the huge estates that looked after their servants in their dotage. Gillian Tripp remembers Mina, a loyal housemaid to her Aunt Tibby and Uncle John in a large house in Greenock, near Glasgow. 'Every night, for as many years as we children could remember, Mina waited at the table in a black dress and white cap and apron,' she recalls. 'Even when she was quite old, Mina spent hours of her life carrying trays of heavy dishes up from the kitchen. She also lit all the beautiful gas chandeliers all over the house every night. After Tibby and John died the house was sold and, out of the proceeds, the family bought Mina a flat in Greenock.'

Nursery nurses who had raised generations of the same family were most likely to be treated well in retirement. Children growing up in the upper classes in the late nineteenth and early twentieth centuries saw more of the family nurse than their own parents and a close bond was formed well into adulthood. As such, they often remained within the household or nearby, in a flat or cottage provided by their one-time charges.

Lady Astor had a strong bond with her children's nurse, known as Nannie Gibbons, and described her as 'my strength and stay and the backbone of my home. She was with us forty years, until she died. She had, I often think, every virtue, and added to them one that is not always found in Nannies – she was utterly and absolutely loyal to me.'

Author Noel Streatfeild remembered the old nurse who had brought up her father and his nine brothers and sisters and lived out her remaining days in the nursery rooms at her grandfather's house. 'She had been married, but her husband had died and so she adopted my father's family. She was a great character, and extremely proud of her nurslings.'

As they grew up, many of her young charges took jobs abroad. 'When they came on leave, almost before they had greeted their parents, they were up the stairs and flinging their arms round old Nannie's neck. As each of the boys became engaged to be married, before the engagement was announced, the fiancée was brought to Nannie for inspection, and she would look them up and down and always ask the same question: "Can you needle?"'

When this charming character died she was buried in the church near the family home. Although it was quite a distance the boys refused to let her travel in a hearse. 'Instead they whom she had carried in her arms, carried her to her grave on their shoulders.'

With no old-age pension or sick pay, staff had to think ahead and save for the future. Although their wages were a pittance, with all meals and accommodation provided those servants who never married but stayed in service for decades often accumulated a surprisingly large nest egg. One long-serving gardener at Erdigg in Wales amassed £4,000 over his lifetime and a maid, if careful, could stockpile up to £500.

Some large houses provided annuities when servants retired and often these were made as a condition in a will.

Butler to the Earl of Sandwich

Edward Montagu, the 8th Earl of Sandwich took his duty of care to his servants to a whole new level. In 1907 his butler, George Andrews, had a serious operation for a tumour on his spine at a hospital in Queen's Square, London. The Earl was a believer in spiritual healing and visited the sick man, as he recalled later in his memoirs, published in 1919.

My footman, who had been to see him, told me his agony was so great that he could not remain in the room with him. I went off at once to see him and found him lying in a ward adjoining the theatre. While I was talking with Andrews about a visit he had received the day before from the Duchess of Albany, he suddenly said, 'Oh my lord, this agony is returning. It is more than I can bear.' The intuition came to me to say that he was not going to have the return of his pain. I began talking to him about his schooldays etc. He remained free from pain and had no return of it. The nurse was much surprised.

The Earl, who believed this was the first demonstration of his healing powers, treated his butler daily for about four months. 'His improvement was marvellous. He became cheerful and was able to walk about, and lived for a year and nine months.'

For example, Lord Northwick left annual payments of £5 for his butler, under-butler, groom, coachman and nurse which were to be forfeited if invested in a public house. He also left a lump sum of £100 to each member of staff who had been in his service for a year at the time of his death.

Constitutional expert Alastair Bruce worked with the cast of *Downton Abbey* as they filmed at Highclere Castle in Berkshire, which is still the family home of the Earl and Countess of Carnarvon. 'If you worked in a house like this and were well behaved, your position was pretty secure,' he remarked. 'And if you were a good retainer, you could assume that when you retired, you would be put into one of the cottages on the estate and the family who had grown to respect you, like you and possibly even love you – that tentacle of care went on until the day that you were buried in the family graveyard.'

CHAPTER NINE

The High Life

A LTHOUGH LIFE BELOW stairs was tough, there was some fun to be had in the short periods when the domestic staff wasn't rushed off its feet. In the large houses this was often known as 'The High Life' and would consist of a few servants, mostly male, playing cards, gambling or drinking together. For both sexes there would be conversation, practical jokes, laughter and often music. Many servants played instruments, such as fiddles, and a piano was often provided in the servants' hall by kinder employers.

Jean Hunt told author Frank Dawes, 'I can well remember standing at the top of the "kitchen stairs" in my grandmother's Welsh home and listening to gales of laughter coming from down in the kitchen . . . Although they did not go out in the evenings and didn't have a radio or television, they seemed to enjoy themselves.'

Dances

Former footman Eric Horne recalled a particularly happy posting in the castle of an earl where the staff was permitted monthly dances. 'Servants seldom wanted to leave that place, unless they had been there some time and wanted promotion,' he said. 'I think what kept them together to a great extent was that we were allowed a dance on the first Tuesday of every month. The mason who worked on the estate played the cello, his son played second fiddle, the tailor played first violin. I played sometimes as well. Our programme consisted of lancers, quadrilles, waltzes, schottisches, polkas, Valse of Vienna, Mazurka and country dances.'

Servants in big enough households could look forward to servants' balls, thrown by the master and mistress as a treat for their hard-working staff. On these occasions, the tables were turned and the family were expected to wait on the staff although, in reality, outside waiters were usually hired. Cakes, sandwiches, fruit and nuts were laid on along with wine and beer and, in more liberal households, maids were allowed to invite 'serious and regular followers'.

At the Duke of Portland's estate, Welbeck Abbey, the indoor and outdoor staff came to over 250 people and, every year, an orchestra and fifty waiters were brought in from London for the servants' ball.

SEX AND SEDUCTION

According to Angela Lambert's book *Unquiet Souls* , 'When the flamboyantly high-spirited, extravagant Edward Horner seduced Lady Cunard's beautiful, young parlourmaid in 1906, after a drunken lunch, the fourteen-year-old Diana [Manners] thought it "eighteenth century and *droit de seigneur* and rather nice."' The term *droit de seigneur,* literally the 'right of the Lord', harks back to an ancient abomination which gave a feudal lord the right to have sex with his subordinate's bride on her wedding night and the use of it by this young aristocratic lady sums up the attitude of the upper classes to the predatory sexual behaviour which often ruined the life of a vulnerable maid.

Leaving home in their teens with little knowledge and no experience of sex, young maids became easy prey to the men of the household. While the mistress of the house imposed rules to stop those in her employ 'fraternizing' with outsiders or even their own colleagues, in order to 'protect their morals', they often did little to prevent the forceful sexual advances of their own husbands and sons. Far away from home, and sleeping in unlocked rooms, the girls were frequently cajoled or bullied into sharing their bed with a combination of threats, promises and even rape. And yet if a maid fell pregnant, the blame fell squarely on her shoulders and meant instant dismissal, with no references.

Margaret Powell shared a room with an under-parlourmaid named Agnes, who found herself in 'the family way'.

'In those days it was slam the door, dismissal with no money, your own home probably closed to you, nothing left but the street or workhouse,' wrote Margaret. So shameful was her condition, that her loyal friends helped her in her attempts to lose the baby with 'bottles of pennyroyal pills, which were supposed to be very good at getting rid of it, Beecham's pills and quinine. But all they did for Agnes was make her spend half a day on the lavatory.' She also tried hot mustard baths, carrying heavy weights, lifting heavy furniture and jumping on and off a park bench on her day off. But these desperate measures were all to no avail and she was dismissed by the mistress, Mrs Cutler. 'Although Madam told her to leave at the end of the week she did give her a month's wages. But the very fact she did this convinced me in my suspicions as to who the father was . . . I suspected it was a nephew of Mrs Cutler's. He was very young and a very handsome man. He had such an attractive voice that even to hear him say good morning used to make you feel frivolous.' The lad in question had been caught several times on the 'back stairs' and, despite Mrs Cutler's obvious suspicion, it was the remaining female staff that got the lecture in morals.

Of course many girls, perhaps including the unfortunate Agnes, were willing bed partners but while the family member got on with their life, the consequences for the maid were disastrous.

In the smaller houses too, the maids were often the subject of unwanted attention, although some managed to escape unharmed. Connie Edgerton worked for an older gentleman named Mr Huddleston and was thrilled when he bought her some soft kid gloves.

'They were very nice gloves, so I thanked him. But the next time I threw them back at him because he wanted me to go with him,' she revealed to Max Arthur. 'Well this old fellow, he didn't want to take no for an answer and every time from then on he started chasing me round this big oval table in the middle of the room. I used to set off and he would be running after me. I've had him on the floor many a time because he used to fall on the slippery floor and as soon as he fell, I ran out.'

LOVE AND MARRIAGE

Although the class structure was rigid, there were rare stories of distinguished gentlemen marrying their maids. In the nineteenth century, Sir Harry Featherstonhaugh, 2nd Baronet, fell for dairymaid Mary Ann Bullock, after hearing her sing on his estate at Uppark in Sussex. After promoting her to head of the dairy he popped the question to the astonished girl and told her, 'Don't answer me now, but if you will have me, cut a slice out of the leg of mutton that is coming up for my dinner today.' When his meal arrived, a slice was missing, and the engagement was official.

Before their wedding Mary Ann was sent to Paris where she learned to read, write and embroider. Despite an age difference of fifty years and a huge social divide, the couple apparently enjoyed a happy twenty-year marriage, until the Baronet's death aged ninety-two.

Another touching love story involved barrister and civil servant Arthur Munby, who chanced upon the aforementioned maid Hannah Cullwick in the service of a London household and fell in love. The couple secretly courted for eighteen years before he plucked up the courage to tell his father, who was so outraged and ashamed that Arthur never mentioned it again. When they finally married, it was in secret and, although they lived together in the Temple, Hannah behaved as his servant whenever he had company.

Mind the Gap

Earl St Maur, heir to the 12th Duke of Somerset, had a long-term relationship with a kitchen maid called Rosina Swan, who accompanied him on his travels around the world and bore him two children, Harold and Ruth. During his lifetime the Earl paid for a house with servants for them to live in and, on his deathbed, when Harold was a baby, he asked the family to look after them. Ruth married into the Duke of Portland's family and Harold, who would have been the next duke had his parents married, spent many years trying to prove they had wed in Holland, to no avail.

ROMANCE BELOW STAIRS

With little time to leave the house, many of the domestic servants saw few outsiders on a day-to-day basis, bar delivery boys and tradesmen. Hardly surprising then that romance often sprung up between the male and female members of staff. In the large houses, the hierarchy among servants even extended to flirting, as Margaret Thomas found out.

'The housemaids always favoured the footmen but we in the kitchen didn't care for them, for they used to stand silently, criticising us, tapping out a tattoo on the table if we weren't ready with their meals,' she revealed. 'We in the kitchen found our friends among the outdoor staff. We didn't go out much.'

A former third housemaid in Lincolnshire in 1913 told Frank Dawes how she caught the eye of a superior servant. 'The butler gave me more than one kiss as we passed on the back passage upstairs. I used to smile at him if he came in the servants' hall to complain about the noise after supper. The head housemaid said, "How dare you smile at the butler." I think he was always afraid of me giving him away. I never did.'

Although mistresses did their utmost to prevent romance below stairs, they could be generous where marriage was concerned. Jean Hibbert worked at the Duchess of Richmond's house in Goodwood, where she fell for her future husband Spencer, the head gardener. When the pair handed in their notice, as was the custom when marriage was to take place, the Duchess, 'knowing my family were far away and very poor, offered to organize and pay for the wedding from Goodwood House,' she said in her memoirs. The family laid on 'a magnificent spread and lovely wine which the Duke gave us as his present and a fine three-layered wedding cake. The kitchen had been working hard and in secret because I knew nothing about it.'

Most cooks and housekeepers remained unmarried and childless but there were exceptions. In 1927, the cook at Crathorne Hall in Yorkshire married a groom, Albert Davidson. She handed in her notice so that she could devote herself to married life but the family felt they needed her and requested that she return. Mrs Davidson remained the family cook for another thirty years.

Although the majority of the indoor staff was expected to remain single in order to stay in service, the gardeners and gamekeepers, who had cottages on the grounds, often had families. A letter to perspective employee George Inch, from the Revd Donald M. Owen in the late nineteenth century, offered the position of gardener and groom and advised that this came with a furnished cottage for his family and dinner every day in the kitchen of the big house. But the letter ended with a surprising condition: 'Of course you would have to reduce your number of children before your wife moved.'

MISTRESSES AND MAIDS

AS WITH THE COMMANDER OF AN ARMY, or the
leader of any enterprise, so is it with the mistress of a house.
Her spirit will be seen through the whole establishment; and
just in proportion as she performs her duties intelligently
and thoroughly, so will her domestics follow in her path.

Mrs Beeton's Book of Household Management

The 'spirit' of the mistress was indeed of huge importance
to the domestic staff as her temperament and generosity
could make the difference between a happy existence and a
miserable one. The Duchess of Richmond, for example, was
considered an excellent employer because she threw wonderful
Christmas parties for her staff and often treated the maids to an
afternoon's theatre, followed by tea at the top-notch Grosvenor
House Hotel.

Margaret Powell remembered a mistress called Mrs Cutler
who used to reward the maids for their efforts in spring-cleaning
with a trip to the theatre. 'But I didn't really enjoy it because
we were in the expensive seats, sitting among the well-to-do,
and I felt conspicuous wearing a somewhat shabby black coat
and a pair of black cotton gloves which I didn't dare take off
because my hands were all red and raw.'

Treats aside, the most frequent complaint about mistresses
was meanness. Even in the big houses, where sumptuous feasts

were served upstairs on a daily basis, some were prone to penny-pinching when it came to feeding the servants. And in smaller houses, where economies had to be made in order to hang on to the status symbol of servants at all, it could be even worse.

When Margaret Powell took her first cook's position at the age of eighteen, she was shocked to find her new mistress was, in the words of a housemaid, 'Mean as a muck-worm, eyes like a gimlet and a nose like a bloodhound.' If the cook let the fire dampen and used the gas stove instead, she would appear at the top of the stairs and demand an explanation. She insisted on ordering supplies herself and, every morning, she marched into the kitchen and inspected the icebox, bread bin, vegetable rack and flour bin before making her list. She also had a locked store cupboard and 'everything was doled out to me in minute quantities. I was never given a key.'

After learning her trade in the generous kitchen of Mrs Cutler's home, Margaret was 'absolutely dumbfounded. I kept imaging Mrs Bowchard's face if Mrs Cutler had come down and done the same thing. She wouldn't have stayed five minutes, she would have given her notice there and then.'

In a letter to author Frank Hawes, one former maid recalled working in a household for several years, before and after the First World War, in which the ladies gave the maids their cast-off clothes – and then docked their wages to pay for them. While the main house was wired for electricity, a candle was still considered adequate in the maids' rooms. Another London maid recalled being allowed half a pound of cheese a week, 'But I mustn't have their cheese – I had the cheaper cheese.' Butchers also sold 'servants' bacon', which were cheaper offcuts than the prime rashers served to the family.

Not all mistresses were monsters, however, and, with the social changes in the early part of the twentieth century, maids began to be seen as valuable help, rather than inhuman goods and chattels. In the smaller houses, some were even helped in their tasks by their mistress.

In memoirs jotted down for her family, Jean Cook remembered her grandmother's house in Greenock where Mina, the maid of forty years, a cook and a housemaid were employed. 'After having presided at the head of the breakfast table Granny left at 9.00 on the dot and "took the side of the beds" with the reigning housemaid. Those left in the dining room were treated to the jangle of the chandelier as she went about her task. Then to the basement to consult with the cook and tell the gardener what vegetables would be required. She made a weekly visit to the Black Pudding Shop, which was well off the beaten track.'

CHILDREN OF THE HOUSE

Like the domestic staff, Victorian and Edwardian children were expected to be 'seen and not heard' and were subject to strict rules at all times. They tended to feel some solidarity with those who toiled 'below stairs' and, as a result, the basement held a great deal of fascination.

Mrs Edith Melville-Steele reminisced about her family servants between 1890 and 1920 in a letter to Frank Dawes. 'Despite the great social differences we were genuinely fond of them, in a special sort of way, of course. I remember my brother and I pleading with mother to allow us to have tea in the kitchen with the maids. This privilege was granted to us only about once a month.'

Sir Osbert Sitwell, in his autobiography *Left Hand! Right Hand!*, stated, 'Parents were aware that the child would be a nuisance and a whole hedge of servants, in addition to the complex guardianship of nursery and schoolroom, was necessary, not so much to aid the infant but to screen him off from his father and mother.' He continued, 'Children and servants often found themselves in league against grown-ups and employers.'

Sally Cook recalled she and her sister Gill seeking the company of her aunt's housemaid and cook in their Greenock house. 'They lived in the basement which was dominated by a huge cooking range and upstairs, in the butler's pantry, Mina made the most beautiful Melba toast – acres of it every week. We loved to go down to see them but we had to wait to be invited to the basement because it was the servants' home and it would have been rude just to barge in.'

Gill added, 'Instead of a servant bell there was a whistle in the butler's pantry inserted into a tube. You whistled and a maid would speak into the tube from the kitchen downstairs. We loved this and probably drove Mina mad.'

GOSSIP

Cassell's Household Guide cautions against the use of charwomen because 'the love of gossip is inherent in the class, and the affairs of every one of the families the charwoman serves become in most cases a common fund of conversation. Domestic matters of the most delicate nature are discussed, and in an unsparing manner.' It adds: 'Whatever facts are not accurately known are unhesitatingly surmised, until all privacy of living is out of the question with whatever neighbours may happen to be at the mercy of the same ignorant tongue.'

The same could be said of many of the staff below stairs, however, and mistresses lived in fear of the family's business being broadcast through the staff grapevine that ran from one large house to another. Even without the staff leaving the house, a titbit gleaned by the footman at the dinner table could be carried to the maids, who might well repeat it to the lad delivering milk or butter, ensuring it would reach every back door in the vicinity. And by the time it had reached the ears of the mistress's society friends, Chinese whispers could have blown it into something truly shocking.

As an innocent young kitchen maid, Margaret Powell heard the most outrageous stories from the visiting driver of a horse-drawn hackney carriage. He would amuse the cook Mrs McIlroy with the goings-on of the folk in the big house nearby. 'I listened all agog,' she wrote. 'Well, according to this Ambrose Datchett, the most outrageous affairs used to go on in this household and, strangely enough, not so much among the women servants but between the footman and stewards and the people upstairs; not only the people who owned the house but the visitors too. Once I heard Mrs McIlroy say, "Not her Ladyship!" Ambrose Datchett said, "I saw it with my own eyes." So Mrs McIlroy says, "What, with her?" "Her, and with him too," he said. "He's a handsome young man." I gathered it was one of the footmen having an affair with both the Lady and the Master of the house.'

While working at Goodwood House, Jean Hibbert was told some scandalous tales regarding another big house in the area, called West Dean, where 'the morals of the guests were supposed to be so loose that the garden boy had to ring the bell fixed at the corner of the house at 6 a.m., called "the change beds bell" so that housemaids would find the right husbands and wives together in bed when they delivered their morning tea at 7!'

Many of these stories were blown up out of all proportion but there's no doubt that the Edwardian upper crust had double standards when it came to their own morals and those of their servants.

Even in middle-class homes a family's social status was all-important and mistresses were ever fearful that their maids might expose them as being less than perfect. Rose Trinder remembered an aunt who lived in Bromley who was desperate to keep her working-class roots from her maid. 'We were allowed to visit the day the maid was out – to keep class, you see. She wouldn't have it known that she knew us people that lived in Deptford or New Cross.'

Conclusion

THE SERVANT PROBLEM

A TTITUDES TOWARDS SERVITUDE had already begun to change by the turn of the twentieth century, with women in particular finding opportunities in shops, factories and offices more attractive and less enslaving. The '£20 maid' was hard to come by. Pay demands had increased and a National Insurance tax, introduced in 1911, meant both mistress and maid had to contribute 3*d*. a week to cover potential illnesses. Many middle-class homes could no longer afford to keep servants, or were forced to reduce numbers, and even the big houses felt the need to economize. Writing in his diaries in 1915, Colonel James Stevenson observed:

> *The lower orders have a great deal of money – more*
> *than they ever had before. The landowners are those who*

suffer as their rents remain the same – taxes enormously increased and very much higher wages have to be paid to servants on account of competition of public bodies, county councils, parish councils etc., who are most extravagant in the wages they give – not having to pay them themselves.

But it was the outbreak of the First World War which really sounded the death knell for domestic service, at least to the extent it had flourished before. Many of the younger male servants enlisted while the women found themselves jobs filling the vacancies left by men fighting abroad. Throughout the UK, 400,000 people left service and the government and press urged employers to let their staff go. *Country Life* magazine ran an article in January 1915 which asked 'Have you a Butler, Groom, Chauffeur, Gardener or Gamekeeper serving you who, at this moment, should be serving your king and country? Have you a man preserving your game who should be preserving your country?'

On their return from the front, fewer men were prepared to enter the life of servitude that the 'lower orders' had once seen as a privilege. In his memoir *From Hallboy to House Steward,* Willam Lanceley commented that the war work many were asked to do 'was a novelty to them, the pay was big and they had short hours, hundreds being spoilt for service through it. It made those who returned to service unsettled.'

In 1919, the Women's Advisory Council presented a report on the 'Domestic Service Problem' to Parliament, which concluded that 'there is amongst girls a growing distaste for domestic service under its present conditions, and a reluctance on the part of parents to allow them to take up such work'. The report suggested proper training and the creation of 'clubs' that would lead to the formation of trade unions, an idea that even some of its own members found unpalatable. The Marchioness of Londonderry refused to sign the section because, she felt, 'any possibility of the introduction into the conditions of domestic service of the type of relations now obtainable between employers and workers in industrial life is extremely undesirable and liable to react in a disastrous manner on the whole foundation of home life'. Others believed the recommendations didn't go far enough because, while they called for reduced hours, fixed breaks for meals and two weeks' paid annual leave, hours and wages would not be enshrined in law.

Historically, mistresses disliked being told how to treat their servants but committee member Dr Marion Philips argued, 'I believe that the reason why it is difficult to get servants today is not lack of training, but because servants are dissatisfied with the wages and hours of work. They are also dissatisfied with many matters which may roughly be classified as questions of social status.'

From 1920, the government attempted to coax young women back into domestic service by running home craft courses, with the condition the pupil would then become a servant, and even offering to pay for the uniforms required to enter a first position. But a life of servitude no longer held any appeal to the majority of women and the days when life below stairs provided the only way out of crushing poverty were for ever gone.

Sources and Bibliography

Max Arthur, *Lost Voices of the Edwardians: 1901–1910 in Their Own Words* (Harper Collins, 2007)

Jane Beckett and Deborah Cherry (ed.), *Edwardian Era* (Phaidon Press, 1987)

Mrs Beeton's Book of Household Management (Oxford, 1861)

Frank Victor Dawes, *Not in Front of the Servants: A True Portrait of Upstairs, Downstairs Life* (Pimlico, 1989)

The Footman's Directory and Butler's Remembrancer (Pryor Publications, 1823)

Jessica Gerard, *Country House Life: Family and Servants, 1815–1914* (Wiley-Blackwell, 1995)

Gareth Griffiths and Samuel Mullins, *Cap and Apron: Oral History of Domestic Service in the Shires, 1890–1950* (Leicestershire Museums, Arts & Records Service, 1986)

Hints to Domestic Servants, by a Butler in a Gentleman's Family (1854)

Pamela Horn, *Life Below Stairs in the Twentieth Century* (Sutton Publishing, 2003)

Frank E. Huggett, *Life Below Stairs* (John Murray, 1977)

Helen Long, *The Edwardian House* (Manchester University Press, 1993)

Manners of Modern Society (Cassell, Petter and Galpin)

Janet McKenzie Hill, *A Guide To Edwardian Servants* (1922)

Charles Morris, *The Home Cyclopedia Of Cooking And Housekeeping* (W.E. Scull, 1902)

Jeremy Musson, *Up and Down Stairs: The History of the Country House Servant* (John Murray, 2009)

Margaret Powell, *Below Stairs* (Peter Davies, 1968)

Pamela Sambrook, *Keeping Their Place: Domestic Service in the Country House* (The History Press Ltd, 2007)

Noel Streatfeild (ed.), *The Day Before Yesterday: Firsthand Stories of Fifty Years Ago* (Collins, 1956)

Albert Thomas, *The Autobiography of Albert Thomas, Butler at Brasenose College, Oxford* (Michael Joseph, 1944)

Laura Wilson, *Daily Life in a Victorian House* (Puffin, 1998)

Websites
www.accidentalsmallholder.net
www.alexanderpalace.org
www.brighton-hove-rpml.org.uk
www.hinchhouse.org.uk
www.nationalarchives.gov.uk
www.ourwardfamily.com
www.pbs.org/wnet/1900house

Picture
Acknowledgements

Index